The Developing World. Religion One: *From Fear to Faith.*

Co-ordinated in this series with Geography One: *Man Alone;*
History One: *Man Makes His Way;* Science One: *The Science of Man*
Developing the global theme of men learning and living together.

KU-472-972

The Developing World

Devised and Edited by R. Pitcher

Religion One

From Fear
to Faith

B. Wigley, B.A., B.D., Dip Ed. Studies
Senior Lecturer in Religious Studies, Eaton Hall College of Education
and

R. Pitcher, Dip. Ed.
Lecturer in Education, Alsager College of Education, Alsager College of Education,
formerly Head of Remedial Department,
Ashfield Comprehensive School

LONGMAN

LONGMAN GROUP LIMITED
Longman House
Burnt Mill, Harlow, Essex CM20 2JE, England
and Associated Companies throughout the World.

© Longman Group Ltd 1969

All rights reserved; no part of this publication may be
reproduced, stored in a retrieval system or transmitted in
any form or by any means — electronic, mechanical,
photocopying, recording or otherwise — without the prior
written permission of the Publishers

First published 1969
Thirteenth impression 1985

ISBN 0 582 21491 2

Illustrated by Bernard Brett

Produced by Longman Group (FE) Ltd
Printed in Hong Kong

Contents

Unit 1
Ghostly Magic

When the Russian astronaut Yuri Gagarin was launched into space on 12 April 1961, he reported back that he could not see God anywhere 'up there'. But what could he have expected to see? A white haired old man or a thunderous great person?

From the earliest days people have sensed that there must be a mighty force somewhere which is far greater than any ordinary person. As people have tried to find out what this mysterious force is like they have had all sorts of strange ideas. But how could they describe something which they could not see? Could it be like a great king or a powerful animal, or even something entirely different?

Early Ideas about Spirits and Gods

Primitive people rarely believed in one god but in many gods. Also their thoughts about these gods varied from time to time. Every country had its own special gods to protect it from its enemies.

At first, they just thought of gods as shadowy spirits. They thought that anything which looked strange or weird contained a 'spirit'. Even a strangely shaped tree root or coloured stone would be treasured because men believed that these objects could bring good luck and protect them from evil 'spirits'. They were thought to have the power to charm away these evil spirits. These special lucky charms, as they were called, were also known as FETISHES.

For example, the Ngbaka women of the North Congo had glass bead fetishes. The beads were tied in a special way along the front of a baby's head in order to frighten or chase away the evil spirits. Similarly, the Saxons buried wolves' feet near their houses to drive away such spirits. The stone, bead or any other weird object was believed to have its own special spirit. This belief that spirits live in such objects as stones, tree roots, and mountains is called ANIMISM.

It has been fairly common throughout the world for man either to bury his dead along with precious personal possessions under trees. Therefore in many places trees became local shrines or holy places. But as people learned more they began to think that spirits could live even in animals. Since observant hunters admired a lion's courage, they would carve statues of lions, wear lion tattoos, drink lion's blood, and wear lion masks in an attempt to persuade the spirit that gave the lion courage to make *them* courageous.

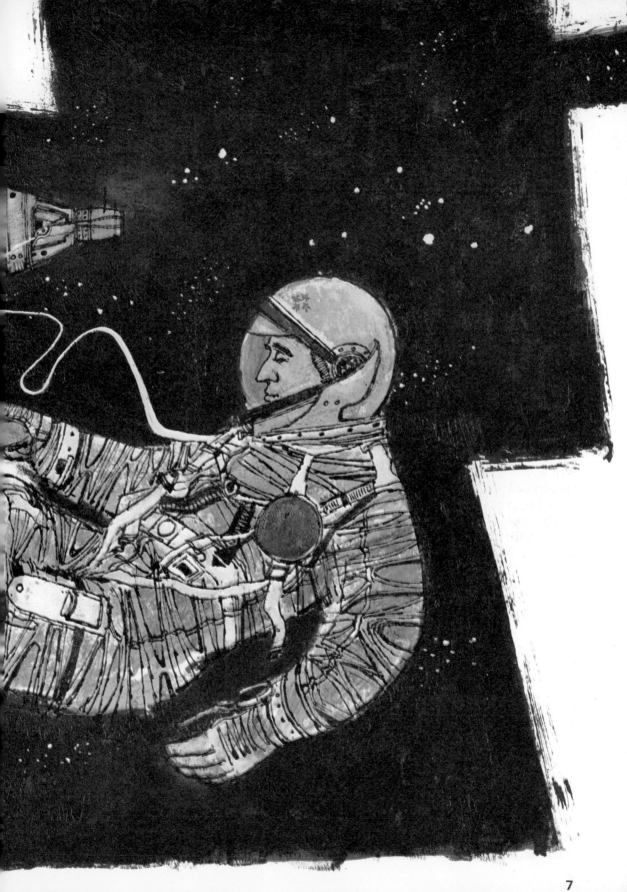

Fear of Death

Many people today claim that they are afraid not so much of death as of dying. In spite of the colossal achievements of science and medicine, man is still no nearer to solving the riddle of death. All created things decay and die. The Psalmist knew this when he said, 'My days are like an evening shadow; I wither away like grass.' *Psalm 102: v 11. (See also Isaiah 40: v 6–8).*

Similarly in the past no one could understand death and most primitive tribes were frightened by it. A dead body or a dead animal may cause primitive people to have nightmares. They were convinced that in their dreams it was really the spirit of a dead man or animal that had come back to haunt them. This was one reason why many people used to worship their ANCESTORS.

2

Before China became a Communist country in 1949 people worshipped their ancestors. A Chinese family was thought to consist of the dead as well as of the living. A Chinese man also thought that all his property belonged to the 'dead' members of his family as well as the 'living' ones. They built little shrines in their homes, made out of small stones to remind them of their dead ancestors. If a family was very poor it used pieces of paper instead of stones for the shrine. The Chinese believed that the more attention they paid to their ancestors the kinder would their ancestors' spirits be towards them in dreams. There was usually an important festival in the springtime when every family cleaned their ancestors' graves, repainted parts of it and made offerings of food and money.

2 Ancestor worship in China
3 The power of Nature

In some places the reverse was believed to happen. For instance, the Manus tribe of New Guinea believed that everybody possessed a spirit which they called the MWELOLO. This Mwelolo allowed a person to live a normal healthy life. But if a person forgot to show his respect to the ancestral ghosts they could take away his Mwelolo, that is, the vital essence of his life and he would fall ill. The Manus also believed that these ancestral ghosts could even kill a person if they wanted to, but they did not believe that this happened normally. If it happened at all it was not regarded as true religion but as a kind of black magic. So each Manus person had a protective ghost who was either a dead father or a close relative. In the Old Testament the idea of a guardian angel is only found in its simplest form, but it may be possible to link up this general Jewish idea of a guardian angel with the Manus idea of a 'Sir' or protective ghost. This kind of angel is said to protect human beings from harm. It seems that a person could talk to his guardian ghost only through some other person. This may possibly be the reason why the witch doctors and holy men evolved.

TASK A

1   Make a list of everyday happenings that people are still not able to understand and which may persuade them to believe that there must be a greater force than themselves; e.g. the sudden death of a healthy young man.
2   Four Red Indian tribes used a snake, a buffalo, a bear, and an eagle as their own 'spirit' leaders. Since each of these animals behaves in different ways how do you imagine this would have affected the way in which the four tribes lived?

TASK B

Look up these verses in the Bible and see what they say 'angels' did: *Matt. 1: v 20; Matt. 2: v 13; Luke 1: v 11–14; Luke 1: v 19–22; Acts 5: v 19 and 20; Acts 8: v 26; Acts 12: v 7–11.*

As well as believing in lucky charms, ghosts or spirits that dwelt in stones, trees, mountains, sand and streams, man has also believed in the power of MAGIC. Terror, fear or wonder struck into his heart when he saw lightning strike a tree and set it ablaze, or when a hurricane uprooted houses. It was a kind of magic to him. It happened, he thought, because the spirits were angry and were taking revenge on the people. Erupting volcanoes and terrible thunderstorms were to him the frightening voices of these unknown spirits.

TASK C

1   What would be the effects, good and bad, on a family who worshipped their ancestors? (*Clue:* sad or happy).
2   Many people claim to have seen ghosts. Do you think ghosts exist?
3   Do you know of any local ghost stories? If so, write them down in your own words.

3

Controlling the Spirits

Early man began to think that if someone could perform 'magic' and become powerful enough, he would be able to persuade the 'spirits' to give one tribe victory over an enemy. The person who normally tried to do this became known as the WITCH DOCTOR or SHAMAN. These witch doctors, as we usually call them, were really very clever people who had learned a great deal about life and the ways of nature.

A clever child in a tribe would soon be picked out and trained by the old witch doctor. He learnt how to forecast the weather from signs in the sky and how to interpret actions of certain animals and their effect on the life of the tribe. He also learned how to spot a person who was telling a lie. He paid particular attention to the habits of animals and learned how to make certain medicines out of herbs and plants. Some of the plants used by witch doctors included garlic, cyclamen, squill, quinine, castor oil and wormwood; many of which are still used in modern medicine. The shaman's special knowledge of plants and his ability to act in certain strange ways caused other members of the tribe to fear him and as a result he became very powerful.

There are many people who believe that gypsies have the power to cast spells for good or evil. One of the commonest sights at fairgrounds is that of the gypsies who sit in the doorways of their caravans and offer to tell our fortunes. This they claim to do in many ways: by reading palms, or casting horoscopes, even by seeing the future in a crystal ball.

The medicine man of the San Blas Islanders in the West Indies possessed strange powers of healing. He made his medicines out of herbs, berries, and roots. However, instead of giving the medicine to the patient, he would take a small wooden doll and file pieces off

4 Voodoo sorcerer of Haiti **4**

5 Gypsies telling fortunes

the part of the body where his patient felt greatest pain. The wooden filings were mixed with the medicine in water and the mixture was drunk by the patient. As with most primitive tribes the medicine man muttered a chant suitable for that particular illness. These San Blas Islanders also believed that their medicine man had miraculous powers over storms and that he could walk on the clouds and even descend into the underworld.

Perhaps the best known and most feared kind of witch doctors were the Voodoo sorcerers of Haiti. There are many legends about how they claimed to be able to do impossible things such as to walk through locked doors and change themselves into animals. Some even claimed that they could raise the dead! There were many strange stories about the way these dead people became robot-like Zombies whom it is said remained in a terrible state of living death. But as soon as these Zombies were given some salt all their memories returned. Such stories were probably told to heighten the witch doctor's influence in Haiti and make him even more fearsome to the people.

Indeed, some of these witch doctors claimed to be able to kill people by using their terrible death wish. They only had to suggest something and it seems that the other person would simply lie down and die. Few people had the courage to argue with them!

TASK D

1   Why do you think these witch doctors and priests had such power over their tribe? (*Clues:* children, brainwashed, fear, expect.)

2   The witch doctors still have great authority over their tribes. Who has the authority over us? Is it a good thing?

Learning about God in the Bible

It seems that many people all over the world had some very strange ideas about the power of the unknown spirits. The Bible tells part of the story of how people have gradually learned about God and moved away slowly from these frightening ideas of spirits and magic. It is true to say that, like many other peoples, the Hebrews sometimes returned to these frightening primitive ideas—their development was not at all regular. One of the basic sins of the Hebrews according to the wise prophets of the eighth century B.C. was that the people would insist on returning to these primitive ideas time and time again.

We cannot understand everything in the Bible, but it is clear that in some stories the Hebrew beliefs were, in some ways, similar to those mentioned in this chapter.

6

Elijah and Elisha were two of the most famous prophets in the Old Testament. They lived some 3,000 years ago. Here are some of the strange things Elijah said his God did through him.

1	He stopped the rain.	*(1 Kings 17: v 1)*
2	He made food.	*(1 Kings 17: v 8–16)*
3	He raised a child from the dead.	*(1 Kings 17: v 17–24)*
4	He made rain.	*(1 Kings 18: v 41–46)*
5	He brought down lightning and fire from heaven.	*(1 Kings 18: v 20–40)*
6	He parted the water in the river Jordan with his cloak.	*(2 Kings 2: v 8–12)*

Although in many ways he was similar to these medicine men many believed that he was more than just a clever person who sometimes tricked everybody else. He is said to have fought against all the worst and most primitive savage beliefs of the people around about him. For instance, children were known to have been sacrificed to the local gods. He and other Old Testament prophets firmly taught the people how to overcome their primitive beliefs and move towards a better understanding of God.

TASK E

Some people claim that Elijah was far superior to the witch doctors or medicine men of other nations. Do you think this is so? If so, why?

Jesus the Healer

Even in New Testament times Jews still believed that sick people were ruled by evil spirits called 'demons'. Had they belonged to the Manus tribe they would have thought that sickness was caused by the 'Mwelolo' being taken away from a person. But the Jewish healer would free the person from these evil spirits by calling them out in the name of a more powerful spirit. Jesus is said to have done something very similar when He performed EXORCISMS, that is, when He 'called out' demons in the name of God. Jesus was obviously influenced by the custom of His own day. Some performed acts, as in Jesus's case, to produce faith. There is a story in the New Testament of the blind man who at first was not completely cured by Jesus. When he first opened his eyes he imagined that he saw 'trees walking'. Find out more about this story. What did Jesus do to encourage the man to have faith in Him? What happened when the man was not able to see properly? *(Look up Mark 8: 22–26)*.

TASK F

Look for some more examples of Jesus healing people. Is there anything different about the way He performed these cures and the way the medicine men cured people? Here are a few examples:

Matthew 9: v 1–8		The paralysed man.
Luke	*4: v 33–37*	The mentally ill.
Luke	*6: v 6–11*	The man with the withered hand.
Mark	*5: v 21–24,*	
	v 35–43	Jairus's daughter.

Apart from those mentioned can you think of any more?

Witch doctors and priests were often able to heal because they were much more clever than the ordinary people. Look up such stories as the one about Jesus walking on the water *(Matt. 14: v 22–27)* or Jesus feeding the five thousand *(Mark 6: v 30–45 and John 6: v 1–14)*. Can they be explained, or are they miracles?

TASK G

Turn to *Mark 1: v 21–28*. By referring to this story explain what you consider to be the main differences in the way Jesus controlled people and the way medicine men did.
(*Clue:* f - - r, f - - - h.)

IDEAS TO DEVELOP

Art and Craft

1   Make four pictures to show the ways medicine men learned their trade.
   a   Take a large sheet of white paper (or sugar paper), and divide it up into four equal spaces.
   b   In the four spaces draw your pictures with wax crayons. Use light colours and put them on thickly. Use some white because it will show up well in the end.

6 The supreme sacrifice
7 Elijah—man of God

    c Mix some dark powder paint in water. It must be runny but not too thin.

    d Paint the mixture all over the paper. The paint will run off the wax, leaving a bright picture.

2 Make a model of a witch doctor's mask.

It will need to be life size.

Make the face front with plasticine.

Cover it with papier mache until it is 1 cm thick all over. Build up any special animal features which you think should be on it. When it is dry, paint and varnish it.

Diagrams

Draw in your work book six 5 cm squares. In each one draw a small diagram to show how people's religious ideas have progressed. (Simple stick diagrams will do):

Fear of the wind	Animism	Lucky charms
Witch doctors	Jesus	'Perfect' man

The diagram for 'wind' could show an uprooted tree falling on a person.

Maps

Put a map of the world in your book. Around the edge of the map draw six 4 cm squares. In them draw diagrams to show what happened in six places mentioned in the chapter, e.g. China: a small shrine. Draw arrows from the squares to the correct places on the map.

Chart

People still have fetishes or lucky charms today.

    In your workbook or on a large sheet of sugar paper draw six lucky charms which are quite common today, e.g. a horseshoe.

Living Language

1 Use these words in sentences to show that you know their correct meaning.

primitive	charm	shrine
spirit	ancestors	ritual

2 From these words try to guess why people believed that spirits lived in trees and rivers.

  a
trees	gloom	overhanging	dark
arms	gnarled	voices	

  b
rivers	drown	power	move
noise	flood		

3 Find the difference between the following words:

saga	myth	fairy tale	legend
parable			

4 Here is part of a famous Red Indian story. Complete it for yourself and then act it as a group.

8 Witch doctor 'making' rain

14

The White Buffalo

One day as two SIOUX Indians were out hunting, they saw a beautiful woman dressed in white buckskins. In her hand she carried a pipe made of red stone and wood, with twelve decorative feathers around it. One of the hunters took the woman to his chief, Standing Hollow Horn. As soon as she saw him she gave him the pipe and explained that, if he smoked it, it would unite all the tribe with the Great Spirit. She explained that the red stone stood for the earth and the feathers stood for the birds of the sky. With that she walked away and as she did so she changed into a white buffalo which later became the tribe's sacred animal.

Deductive Work

1   With the help of this picture find out how witch doctors in Africa tried to make rain.

8

Clue Words: Threat   Imitate   Clouds
           Kill   Holy   Sprinkle

2   A witch doctor can perform either black magic or white magic. What is the difference between these two kinds of magic?

Puzzles

Put these words into 10 pairs of words:

Group A Jesus, Saxon, tattoo, Chinese, shaman, squill, Mwelolo, fetish, voodoo, dead.

Group B picture, plant, Manus, walking trees, ancestor, wolf foot, Zombies, witch doctor, lucky charm, shrine.

Library Work

1 Find out all you can about:
    amulets   halloween   taboo   totem
2 Find pictures of the plants mentioned in this chapter. Draw them and see if you can find out their medicinal value.

Discussion

1 What is luck?
2 Do you think superstitions are simply 'wise' ideas that have grown up over the years or just stupid fears?
3 Are witch doctors evil or good?

Bible Research

Use the Revised Standard Version of the Bible. Some passages in it possibly show how the Hebrew people and others had very primitive religious ideas as they slowly learnt about God.

1 Look up these verses and find what the Bible says happened:

NEAR TREES AND SHRUBS
Gen. 35: v 4   Gen. 35: v 8
Exodus 3: v 2–4   Judges 4: v 4–5
1 Sam. 14: v 2

NEAR MOUNTAINS
1 Kings 18: v 20–40   Gen. 12: v 6–8
STONES – used in different ways:
Gen. 31: v 44–48
Joshua 4: v 1–9

2 Look up the following references which show other primitive religious ideas.

RAINMAKING
1 Sam. 12: v 16–18   1 Kings 18: v 41–46

MAGIC
Exodus 7: v 8–13   Exodus 14: v 19–30
Exodus 15: v 23–25   Matthew 14: v 22–27
Acts 5: v 1–11   Acts 8: v 9–13

GREAT FEATS
Exodus 14: v 21–31   Joshua 3: v 14–17
Joshua 6: v 12–21

DREAMS
Gen. 28: v 11–22   Gen. 37: v 5–11
Gen. 40: v 5–14   Gen. 41: v 1–33

9 Primitive masks
10 Wonders from the Creator

9

Unit 2
A Simple Question

As men tinker with cars and children break open little toys they often say, 'How does this work? Why won't it go now?' Questions! Questions! Questions! People have always been asking them and when they have not been able to find answers they have usually made wild guesses.

Man has been asking many questions throughout the ages, but it has only been comparatively recently that enough knowledge has been gathered to find probable answers to such questions. In the past the answers given were usually based on the result of observations or were mere guesses based on either faith or fear.

Today, answers to two different types of questions are provided by scientists and religious thinkers. Scientists generally try to find out HOW things happen and religious thinkers try to find out WHY they happen. Here are some of the kind of questions they might ask.

SCIENCE	RELIGION
How did the earth begin?	Why did the earth begin?
How do crops grow?	Why do crops grow?
How do people live?	Why do people live good and bad lives?
How do people die?	Why do people die and what happens after death?

TASK A

1   Think of some questions man has asked for thousands of years, the answers to which have only been learnt in the last fifty years.

Clues: Birds in the sky   Spacemen
Deep sea divers

2   What do you think man's life would have been like had he not asked questions?

There Must Be a Creator

News travels like wildfire! Worldwide television and daily newspapers are ready to use as their headlines any new startling idea or discovery. But in the past travel and news were so slow in circulating that any new ideas took a long time to spread. Most people stayed in their home region and hardly went further than the nearest town or city. Most of our ancestors' ideas and their

10

attempted answers to various problems were coloured by their own particular way of life. However, some experiences were common to all people everywhere. For instance, everyone could see the sun, stars, rain, and experience thunderstorms and natural calamities. Therefore explanations for such natural happenings formed an important part of almost every religion, and all over the world these explanations are strangely similar. One problem which interested most people was the problem of creation, because for this, one has only to ask the question: what came first? So we find that many hundreds of silly creation stories came into being.

The Babylonians believed that the world was created when their 'good' god, Marduk, captured his enemy, the evil goddess Tiamat, in a kind of net and strangled her. When he cut her in half, he made her top half the heavens and her lower half the earth.

11 The Babylonian Universe (left) The Hebrew Universe
12 Inca sun worshippers
13 A symbolic painting of Ra being reborn
14 A scarab beetle

11

Sun Worship

Many thought that the sun was something special since they could feel its warmth. In hot climates, it did great damage to crops and humans if they were exposed too long to it. Almost everybody in the world realised that they depended on the life-giving warmth of the sun. So naturally people in the past thought that the sun must have been closely connected with the creation of life and the world.

12

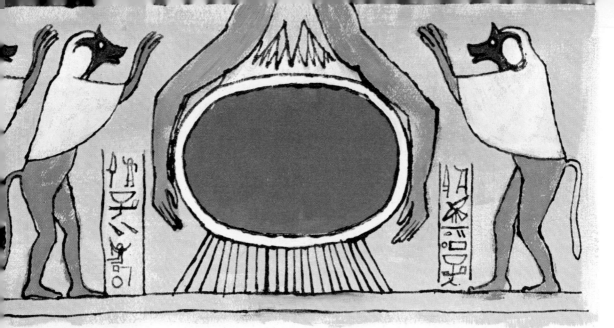

13

Perhaps the most famous of all sun worshippers were the Incas of Peru. They believed that they must not offend the sun. Other people took a similar attitude, and as a result amazing myths grew up about the Sun.

The Egyptians thought of the sun as one of their gods and called it Ra or sometimes Re. They pictured Ra travelling every morning across the sky in a boat. At dawn Ra was very young but by noon he had grown into a full grown man, and by evening time he was so old that he died. During the night, however, Ra sailed under the world in another boat, fighting the spirits of darkness. Whilst Ra was on this night journey he travelled by another name, AUF, which meant a corpse. During this journey, which took twelve hours, he had to fight many battles, but by dawn he was reborn as Ra again.

Some Egyptians even thought that the sun was pushed across the sky by a scarab beetle.

TASK B

14 Find out why the Egyptians thought so highly of the scarab beetle. They used to make amulets in the shape and form of a scarab.

THE HEBREW IDEA OF CREATION

1 Read the first chapter of Genesis. What do you consider to be the biggest single difference between it and the ideas mentioned above?

2 Write down in one sentence what the creation story in Genesis, Chapter 1, is trying to teach.

3 Draw seven 5 cm squares in your workbook. Draw the Hebrew story of creation, stage by stage, in each square. Write under each one a sentence to explain the drawing.

4 How does Science explain how the world was created?

Male and Female Gods

All animal life depends upon there being two sexes. Some people argued that in this world there are two lights. The sun, being the greater light, was like a husband, with the moon, or lesser light, being his wife. We are not surprised therefore to discover that the Maya Indians of Central America chose the moon to be their goddess of childbirth and weaving.

The Egyptians naturally thought of the sun as one of their gods because they lived in a hot climate. The Mesopotamians, however, lived in a frightening stormy climate around the great twin rivers of the Tigris and the Euphrates, and they naturally thought that their gods must be fierce, ugly, and angry, like their weather. They also believed that man was created to be the slave of the gods. Furthermore, unless the gods were given food and wine regularly, the Mesopotamians thought they would be destroyed by floods, disease, or war.

Other tribes and nations such as the Sherpa tribesman of the Himalayan Mountains always had to fight against the overwhelming power of the towering white mountains which even they, as hardened climbers, could not conquer. As the huge irresistible avalanches roared down the slopes, the Sherpas became convinced that these mountains must be the home of powerful gods.

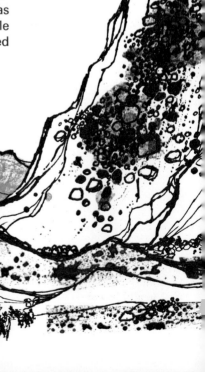

The Eskimos, living in the frozen areas of the north, constantly struggled for survival against the hazards of snow and ice. So naturally they also thought of their goddess, whom they called Sedna, as living under the ice and being responsible for supplying the Eskimos with food of fish and seals.

TASK C

1 Read *Genesis 6: v 11 to 7: v 15* about a famous story which probably originally came from Mesopotamia.
2 What is there in your home area which would have made people think in the past that a god must be near?

17

18

The Gods of Everyday Life

The most important problem for early man was the problem of survival. Natural events such as the growth of crops, storms, and other various calamities of nature which occurred from time to time were thought to have been caused by the gods. Hence early man thought it best to worship these gods and so avoid making them angry, or they would suffer droughts, famines, and earthquakes as punishment.

We have now seen that it was natural for people to liken their gods to their own surroundings. The EGYPTIANS, being farmers, thought that it was their god OSIRIS who first taught man how to use the plough, how to irrigate the land with the shaduf, how to avoid eating poisonous fruits, and even how to make beer.

The MAYA INDIANS of Central America, like the Egyptians, were basically farmers and had similar ideas about the way their gods controlled crops and so on. But their chief interest lay in ASTRONOMY, the study of the sky and stars. Their male god was called ITZAMNA, and he ruled the skies. He was also thought to have invented early signs and 'writing' books. Since the Mayas were astronomers they had one god for the planet Venus and one for the North Star. Their female goddess, called IXCHEL, was responsible for domestic tasks, such as weaving and cooking. Another of their gods, CHAC, was responsible for rain, thunder, and the wind. Chac was also the god of fertility, for the Mayas naturally saw how rain made the crops grow. The Mayas even had a special god to look after their maize.

15 Gods from Mesopotamia
16 A fearful power
17 Sedna
18 A Maya god

The ASSYRIANS of Mesopotamia were a ferocious and warlike people who were happiest when fighting other people. Consequently, their god NERGAL was pictured as being strong, like a bull.

TASK D

Read Byron's poem *The Destruction of Sennacherib*.

Find out more about the Assyrians, e.g. *2 Chron. 32: v 1–22, 2 Kings 18: v 9–37; 19: v 20–34*.

Gods of Good and Evil

Why are some people good whilst others are evil? This question was answered very simply in the past by some people, who said that there must be good and evil gods!

The BABYLONIANS for instance thought of MARDUK as their 'good' god who stood for LIFE and ORDER, whereas his enemy, the goddess TIAMAT was 'evil' and stood for DEATH and CHAOS. These two were constantly fighting each other, and it was this constant battle which accounted for the battle between 'goodness' and 'evil' in the world. The Babylonians were also convinced that the seasons were formed as a result of this battle between Marduk and Tiamat. When it seemed as if Tiamat was winning, the autumn and winter season arrived on earth and everything looked dead. However, when Marduk was winning, and he always seemed to in the end, the seasons of spring and summer caused the crops to reappear and produce a harvest.

Similarly, the IROQUOIS INDIANS thought that the Master of life sent nothing but 'good' things to the earth but unfortunately he had an evil brother with whom he was always at war. During the winter the Iroquois Indian performed dances to help the Master of life to win the struggle against evil, and his victory showed itself every year in the coming of spring.

Evil Spirits of Darkness

The Iroquois Indians also believed that illness was the result of what they called 'False Faces'. These faces were horrible, bodiless heads, which roamed through the dark forests.

The INCAS also believed in bodiless, evil spirits, called SOPAYS. The sopays wandered around at night causing evil events and murmuring as they went along, 'wis, wis; wis, wis; . . .' The priests thought that they could drive these spirits away by blowing tobacco smoke at them.

TASK F

1   We still believe that there is evil in the world. What are the most evil things you know about, and which you know have happened? What caused them?

2 Why do you think it is appropriate to liken evil to darkness? This is done in the Bible. *Look up these references: John 3: v 19–21; John 12: v 46; Romans 13: v 11–13; 1 Thess. 5: v 5–8.*

The Hebrew God

The name Hebrew may refer to nomadic tribes of shepherds called the HABIRU whose leader Abram crossed over the river Euphrates, away from Mesopotamia, because he could not accept the gods of that region. He became convinced that the true living God did not want men to fashion Him in the shapes of animals or man, neither did He want them to offer human sacrifices to Him.

Even the Hebrews were not entirely free from some of the primitive ideas mentioned already about gods. But on rare occasions in their long history certain of their prophets and leaders came to startling conclusions about the one whom they knew as the 'True and Living God'. It has to be made quite clear that not all Hebrews held the following basic beliefs at the same time. However, from time to time these ideas became a dominant part of their faith.

1 The Hebrew God demanded goodness rather than sacrifice, whereas other nations thought that their gods could be bribed into helping them by gifts.

2 Yahweh was the Invisible or Almighty God who created all things.

3 Yahweh was so Holy that no one could look at Him and live.

4 However, Yahweh wanted to save man from evil. He chose the Hebrews as the nation through which He would make himself known to all mankind.

5 He made a Covenant or Agreement between Himself and the Hebrews. If the people obeyed His commandments He would be their God.

6 He promised that one day a MESSIAH or Deliverer would come to release all mankind from evil. This Messiah would show the true nature of God.

19 An Assyrian god

TASK I

1 Look up *Matthew 9: v 9–13.* What does verse *13* mean in connection with the story?

2 Look up *Hosea 6: v 6.* What does Hosea say at this place? Is it any different from what Jesus said?

The Messiah

For centuries Christians claimed unique privilege as far as knowledge of the true living God was concerned, just as the Hebrews, now known as the Jews, claimed to have been given special revelations by YAHWEH, which was their name for God. The Hebrews thought this was the natural result of the Covenant they had made with God when they were chosen by Him to show the way to the rest of the world. However, this chapter so far shows how men were aware from the earliest times that there was someone 'greater than themselves' who ruled over the world. The problem of whether or not the Hebrew and Christian ideas of God are different from others is too complex to study here, but at least one thing is certain. In both the Old and the New Testament it is God who takes the initial step. The Jewish prophets were convinced that they were speaking God's words and their messages began, 'Thus saith the Lord . . .' Similarly, Christians are convinced that Jesus is the Messiah because He was sent by God expressly for the purpose of saving man from death. So when Jesus of Nazareth came, He showed for all time, so Christians claim, that the true living God is not an angry tyrant but a person who is to be thought of as a heavenly Father, who loves all men as a father loves his own children.

From now on Christians are convinced that God is to be obeyed in faith rather than in fear. He is said to give mankind hope. He is no longer to be worshipped as a last resort. He has nothing to do with luck or fate but is a God of Love. Jesus said: 'For God so loved the world, that He gave His only begotten Son, that whosoever believeth in Him, should not perish but have everlasting life.' *(John 3: v 16).*

TASK J

1 Abraham was the founder of the Hebrew race.
   Find out all you can about him from these references:
a Who was Abraham's father? *Gen. 11: v 27.*
b Who was his wife? *Gen. 11: v 29.*
c What was God's first promise to him? *Gen. 12: v 2–3.*
d What did Abraham do when he reached Canaan? *Gen. 12: v 7–8.*
e How did be become a man of fear? *Gen. 12: v 10–20.*
f How did he show himself to be a man of generosity? *Gen. 13: v 5–18.*
g How did he show himself to be a man of courage? *Gen. 14: v 13–16.*
h How did he show himself to be a man of prayer? *Gen. 18: v 22–33.*
i How did he show himself to be a man of obedience? *Gen. 22: v 1–14.*
j What did God promise him? *Gen. 22: v 15–19.*
k Find out when Abram's name was changed to Abraham. *Gen. 17: v 1–5.*
2 Much more can be said about the idea of a Messiah. Try to find out with the assistance of your teacher how the idea of Messiahship evolved.

The MASAI cattle herders of East Afria thought that their god NGAI (pronounced Enkai) was the great god who sent down cattle to earth from the skies on a huge slope made of leather. In the past, when they saw other tribes with cattle they were sure that the cattle had been stolen from their god Ngai and therefore had to be recaptured by them. As a result they were constantly fighting other tribes for cattle.

In these various and interesting ways people looked for gods as the cause and explanation of everything. It has been estimated that the Egyptians had well over 2,000 gods. They are even known to have invented a god for every part of the body and even one to guard their cemeteries.

TASK E

1 Were the people entirely wrong to think that the gods cared and looked after everything? *Look up Matt. 6: v 25–34.*
2 The Israelites were mainly shepherds. How would they have expected God to act? *Read Psalm 23.*
3 In *Isaiah 40: v 10–17* and in *v 28–31* there is a description of what God is like and what He does. Read it carefully and make a list of what this writer believed God to be like. How would you try to describe God?

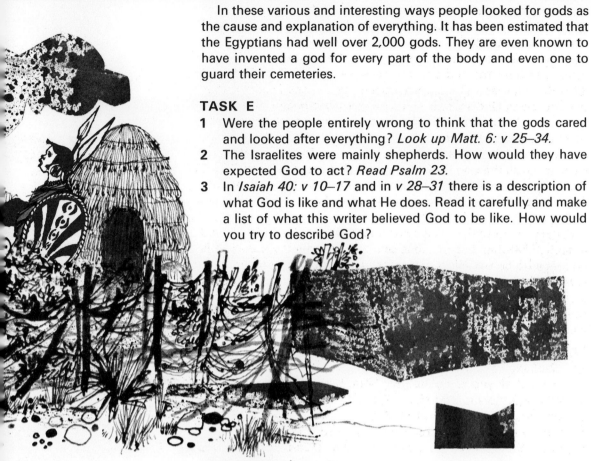

IDEAS TO DEVELOP

Try to do the impossible — paint or make a picture of your idea of God.

Mobile

Make a mobile of *six* of the gods mentioned in this chapter.

Use ordinary wire coat hangers bent in an inverted V shape.

Draw and paint the gods on one side of pieces of card 10 cm square and the name of the god on the reverse side.

Use the top piece for Yahweh: a plain white disc with no face nor any other shape to it. A circle has no end and is a perfect geometric shape. Hang the pictures of the other gods with cottons from the mobile arms.

Diagrams

In the centre of a double page in your work book draw a circle with a radius of 3 cm. Put a small symbol in it to represent God (e.g. a crown) and label it. Around the double page draw six circles with a radius of 2 cm. In each one draw a symbol to show what the Hebrews thought about God. Label each one neatly. Join the six circles to the centre circle with straight lines.

20 Masai receive their herds from Ngai

Charts

Draw a chart to show these animal-type gods, some of which had animal heads. Label each one and state which ones stand for:

strength   fertility   pleasure   sun   family   light

Living Language

1   Use these six words in sentences to show that you know what they mean:

corpse   nomadic   overwhelming
astronomer   observation   unique

2 Pair the correct halves of these six sentences and write them in your book.

a	People thought that gods	with the strongest gods won battles.
b	Every country had	they would fight against enemy gods better.
c	People thought that the nations	they would desert their people.
d	The gods needed to be fed	its own king and gods.
e	If the gods were looked after	were like great people.
f	If the gods were not looked after	just like human beings.

3 Here is a famous Egyptian myth. Read this and make up a play based on it.

Nut, the goddess of heaven, married Sibou, the god of earth. But she did so without the permission of Ra the Sun God. So Ra cast a spell on Nut and said that she would be childless. However another god Thoth took pity on Nut and in a game of draughts with the Moon God managed to persuade the Moon God to provide five extra days in the year. Thoth went and told Nut that she could have children on this special fifty-third week of the year. As a result Osiris was born. Ra soon forgave Nut when he saw his handsome grandson and he later had Osiris to live with him.

Deductive Work

1 The sun was often thought of as the god of life and the moon as the god of time. Why was this so? (*Clue:* orbit).
2 What do you think the gods, called Mazda and Vesta, were supposed to represent? Check your guess.
3 The Inca farmers worshipped the earth. What did the Inca fishermen worship on the coasts of Ecuador?

Puzzle

Here are 10 words found in the unit. What is mentioned in connection with each one?

Scarab beetle	Marduk	Auf	Tigris
Sedna	Astronomy	False faces	Messiah
Darkness	Nazareth		

Library Work

Find out the names of the Roman gods of:

War	Sea	Hunting	Messenger
King of Gods		Queen of Gods	

(*Clues:* Rmas   Tnpeuen   Dnaia   Mrcyrue   Jtrepiu   Nujo).

What do you think they did? Draw 5 cm squares down the edge of two pages in your work book. Draw the gods in the squares and write four lines about each one underneath the picture.

21

21 Toueris, Bes, Mazda, Ra, Nergal, Vesta,

Project

Either

Collect as many different creation stories as possible. Draw and describe them in your book. (*Clue:* Look up these stories using this list of books or any other you can find. *Lost Worlds* Golden Press; *Egyptian Mythology* Paul Hamlyn; Life: *World's Great Religions* Collins.)

Or

Make a study of these Viking gods:

Odin	Tyr
Frigg	Balder
Thor	Hod

What would you have expected the gods of these seafaring warriors to have been like? (See: *Tales of the Norse Gods and Heroes* by B. Picard, Oxford University Press.)

Bible Research

What the Hebrews thought God was like.

1 Why did their prophets tell them not to worship idols? *Isaiah 44: v 9–20; 46: v 5–10; 66: v 1–2.*
2 Who were the Hebrews to worship? *Exodus 20: v 2.*
3 What were the Hebrews to make Him look like? *Ex. 20: v 4.*
4 What did God demand from the Hebrews? *Isaiah 1: v 11–20; Micah 6: v 6–8.*
5 Write out the first four of the Ten Commandments. Put a red box around them and print *Mark 12: v 29* and *30* by their side.
56 Write out the last six commandments. Put a blue box around them and print *Mark 12: v 31* by their side.
7 Jesus had special ideas about God. Look up *John 4: v 24,* and make a list of Jesus's ideas about God.

Discussion

1 What do you think, from what you have read in this chapter, are the main differences between man and the lower animals?

Look carefully at this picture. Many people say that these things can become modern gods. How far is this true?

(*Clue:* cost   time   attention.)

22 Modern gods
23 Henry II being scourged

Unit 3
Middle Men

It was 1174 and the mighty English King was lying there, being scourged by the priests. It was an unbelievable sight, but the citizens of Canterbury had already seen Henry II walk bare footed from St. Dunstan's Church to Canterbury on a pilgrimage to Thomas à Becket's tomb. There, dressed only in a woollen smock, he willingly knelt before the tomb to be scourged and to beg forgiveness for the saint's murder in the Cathedral. He continued to pray all day and night before returning to London.

23

Once the Holy Men organised themselves properly they soon realised that they possessed power over life and death. They found that they could persuade good people not only to sacrifice other human beings but to endure terrible sufferings and even to commit suicide in the name of their mysterious, unknown gods. But it had not always been like that.

In the beginning there were probably neither Holy Men nor Priests. Whilst men were nomadic hunters or herders roaming the country in search of food they just did not have time to think deeply about the mysteries of the spirits. The pigmies today are still like that. When they are in need of the spirits' help, they just light a fire by a tree to make the 'Great Spirit of the Forest' aware of their need. So at first the father of each family or the tribal leader was the only spiritual teacher and he blessed the food, offered simple sacrifices, and said special prayers.

Usually it was only when men ceased to be nomads and became farmers and craftsmen, living in villages and towns, that a special person called a Holy Man appeared in each tribe. As the people tilled the land, collected the harvests, built and repaired houses, they were often too busy to attend to matters of the spirits. Furthermore, the village leaders had to judge the people as well as try to explain the mysteries of the dark forest, the appearance of rain and the growth of the crops.

But in the course of time even the leaders had neither the time nor the energy to delve into spiritual matters. This is probably why a special 'Holy Man' was needed—to give his entire time to the study of these spiritual matters. He was expected to help everyone to overcome their fears and anxieties. We find that many tribes, though, such as the Navaho Red Indians, who thought that sickness and disease were unnatural and the result of 'evil' spirits, had medicine men to explain these mysteries. The medicine man or witch doctor amongst the Asanti tribes of West Africa had to spend three years in the forest studying these mysteries before he could become a Holy Man. Hence the word Holy, which means 'separate', was most suitable for them. So the Holy Man was separated from the tribe to learn the secret ways of the spirits and to act as a MEDIATOR or 'go-between', between the spirits and the people.

24

TASK A

1 In the Bible one of the greatest 'go-betweens' was Moses. From these verses read what kind of things he is said to have done: *Exodus 3: v 11–17; 5–6: v 13; 7: v 14–25; 8: v 5–15; 8: v 16–32; 16: v 1–8.*

2 The above reference to Moses and to the way he acted as a 'go-between' will help you to decide why some people today feel that they need a 'go-between' in their everyday life. (*Clue:* great person.)

3 Make a list of all ten plagues. What do you think really happened? Was it a mere coincidence or do you think that all Moses did was to read the signs of the Egyptian climate?

4 Imagine you are a newspaper reporter. Write out an account of what happened to the people during these plagues.

Types of Holy Men

Although these special holy men were all 'separated' out to discover more about the secret matters of the spirit, it is possible to divide them into four distinct groups. A holy man could be called a witch doctor, a medicine man, a seer, or a priest.

1   The WITCH DOCTOR'S main purpose was to act as a general adviser to the tribe.
2   The MEDICINE MAN had the special task of dealing with sicknesses connected with the mind or body.
3   The SEER was a kind of prophet or gazer into the future. He often proclaimed messages which he said had been delivered to him by spirit gods.
4   The PRIESTS were the temple administrators. Their main function, as we shall see, was to deal with rituals and sacrifices.

Most types of holy men, however, performed many of these tasks at the same time. In the following section, therefore, they have been drawn together for the sake of brevity.

Early Holy Men or Seers

A holy man is also called a SEER. That is a 'see - er' or a person who is able to 'see' and understand omens and signs such as dreams, visions, and strange events such as eclipses and falling stars.

The seers' main task was to convince people that the spirits or gods were on their side. To do this the seers would try to persuade the spirits to obey them by saying special magic words. For example, the Buddhist priests of India would continually repeat the words 'Om Mani Padme Hum', or in short 'Om', in the belief that it would either persuade the gods to give them a message, or help them cure a sick person.

At times these holy men could be in very great danger. The medicine man amongst the Pah Utes Red Indians was a very important person, but if too many of the tribe died he was blamed for their death and killed. The tribes were usually almost at the mercy of the seers, but the strange thing is that these seers seldom tried to make the people live better lives. Nevertheless, the holy men performed useful if often fanciful work.

24 An African tribal priest

The Seers as Rainmakers

The Aztecs of Mexico were entranced by the mystery of rain and one of their main gods was TLALCOC, the god of rain. The priests would chant, 'Oh my lord, magician prince, truly it is to you the maize belongs', and during the month of Tlalcoc children were drowned as offerings, in the hope that this powerful water god would produce rain and help the maize god to cause the maize to grow. (Quoted from *Everyday Life of the Aztecs* by J. Soustelle.)

In the Old Testament

Water was also important to the Hebrews, not only whilst they were nomads wandering in the desert under their leader Moses, but also when they had settled down in Canaan, where drought was not uncommon.

TASK B

1   When Moses took the Hebrews into the desert he was expected to produce water for drinking. Read the following references and explain in what ways, if any, you think Moses is unlike the seers mentioned above.
    (*Clue:* Did he have the people's interest at heart?)
    Exodus 15: v 22–26; Exodus 17: v 1–8.

2   Elijah also made use of water and was expected to make rain. Look up these references:
    God showed special favour to his seer—*1 Kings 17: v 1–8.*
    1 Kings 18: v 20–40.
    2 Kings 2: v 6–12.

25 Life among the Aztecs
26 A terebinth tree

The Seers as Healers

The seers did strange things as they tried to cure sick people who came to them for help. Since sickness was thought to be due to the presence of an evil spirit inside a person, the seer had to call out these spirits, DEMONS, JINNS, GHOULS or VAMPIRES, in the name of a greater and stronger spirit or god. To help the cure the medicine man performed certain acts. For instance, sometimes he sprinkled water over the body; at other times he covered the body with flour; on other occasions a branch from a sacred tree, such as the TEREBINTH mentioned in the Bible, was waved above the person's head. Another common method was to give the sick person a statue of the god to hold, as the seer said magic formulas, doubtless believing that in this way the god's power entered the patient, as he held the stone or wooden statue.

The Incas of PERU thought that pain and death were unnatural. A man was thought to suffer and die simply because VIRACOCHA the sun god, was angry with him. Holy men therefore looked for the causes of death and sickness by inspecting specially inflated llama lungs which they believed contained special signs. When an Inca Emperor died there was terrible suffering. The priests laid the blame on all kinds of animals and people, who were then sacrificed to Viracocha. However, the priests managed to learn in this way how to perform simple surgical operations. Similarly, Sumerian seers, who were called Baru, examined the livers, gall bladders, hearts, kidneys and entrails of sacrificed victims, claiming that certain marks on them were signs from the gods.

Jesus the Holy Man

Although Jesus was a holy man, His methods were completely different. He accepted most of the current beliefs of His day—such as the belief that disease and sickness were caused by evil demons. But he denied that sick people had lost the love and blessing of God as some Jews maintained. His idea of God was that of a Loving Father who cared for all men, *particularly* those who were ill. Another difference between Jesus and the ordinary seer was the fact that he never forced people or frightened them into believing in what He knew as the higher Spirit of God, whom He usually called the Father. He explained to them that the Father loved them and that if only they responded to Him in faith and love they would be healed. Jesus never claimed to be responsible for the cure. He would almost certainly say to the person after the healing: 'Go thy way; thy faith hath made thee whole.' Nevertheless, there is one definite hint in the New Testament that it took tremendous energy or power to perform these cures by Jesus. Look up the story of the healing of the woman with the haemorrhage in *Mark 5: v 24–34*.

TASK C

1   What is the strange feature in this story?
2   'It matters not whether we think a person is possessed by demons, bugs or germs.' Discuss.

26

The Seer as a Spiritual Interpreter and Adviser

'Wise men seek advice, fools say they know.'

Every day we are all faced with problems we find difficult to solve, and although we now have much more knowledge, we still need help from people who have specialist knowledge such as doctors, surgeons, scientists and lawyers.

The greatest so called 'specialists' in the past were the religious holy men. It was not unusual for kings to ask them for forgiveness, or to ask when they should fight against their enemies. So too women pleaded to be given the ability to have children and men went to the holy men seeking justice about arguments over family quarrels. Here are some examples of the way in which seers helped the tribes to make important decisions.

In Egypt the seers, who were called the SUNU, spoke magic words and used magic numbers to help foretell the future. So too, Egyptian mothers recited magic words as they put their children to bed. In such ways mothers hoped to persuade the gods to protect their children at night.

Babylonian seers claimed to be able to predict future events by examining the movements of stars, planets and other heavenly bodies. They had special magic signs for each month of the year. These Babylonian seers also thought eclipses were important and gave special warnings. If an eclipse occurred in the month of Nisan (during March–April) it meant that a calamity would happen. However, if it occurred in the month of Tammuz (June–July) there would be a bumper harvest.

Finally, these seers were advisers and often helped to mould tribes into peaceful communities.

TASK D

1 One of the most famous seers in the Old Testament was Samuel. Turn to these verses and see what he did as:

Battle adviser	*1 Samuel 7: v 3–12.*
Judge	*1 Samuel 7: v 15–17.*
A king maker	*1 Samuel 8: v 4–10 and 22; 9: v 17; 10: v 1.*
Foreteller of the future	*1 Samuel 9: v 6–10 and 20.*
Giver of signs	*1 Samuel 10: v 5–10.*
Religious teacher	*1 Samuel 12: v 14–16.*

2 Are you superstitious? Why do so many people think 13 is an unlucky number? (*Clue:* The Last Supper – see *Luke 22: v 14–23.*)

27 The Last Supper

The Priests

Seers were usually holy men who wandered around teaching about God. But priests generally arose at a later period in time when there were special holy buildings called temples. These priests had duties to perform in temples. Priestly functions were often passed on from father to son in one family or tribe. In the Bible the Jews limited the priesthood to the tribe of Levi. According to *Exodus 40: v 7–75* the priestly office was to be limited to the sons of Aaron.

TASK E

Read *Numbers 3: v 5–12.* What does this tell in addition about the priesthood?

The priests had three main tasks:

1 To accept 'sacrifices' on behalf of the people.
2 To prepare the sacrifice for God. They collected the blood of the animal into special bowls and they 'dressed' the animal which was sacrificed by burning it on ALTARS.
3 They spoke certain words on behalf of the people and asked God to accept sacrifices as a symbol of the people's faith and loyalty.

Priests, like the other holy men, had great influence. It was the priest who decided whether or not a person's sacrifice was acceptable. Furthermore a person's sin could only be forgiven if he offered his sacrifice through the priest. He could not do it himself. If a man was cured from a disease such as leprosy, he had to be given a certificate from the priest to show that he was 'clean' again. I wonder if this is the origin of the phrase 'to have a clean bill of health'?

Another example of the power of priests can be seen at work on the Island of Bali. The Balinese have a temple in the middle of the island, towards which everyone turns at various times during the day. By doing this they are always reminded of their religious faith. Once a Balinese leaves his island, however, and is unable to see his temple and priests, he usually feels so lost that he wants to return home.

TASK F

1 What did lepers have to do as they walked about? *Leviticus 13: v 45 and 46.*
2 How did the priest decide whether a person had leprosy? *Leviticus 13: v 9–44.*
3 What did Jesus tell ten lepers to do? *Luke 17: v 11–19.*
4 Using these clue words decide for yourself if these priests were doing a worth-while job.

    tribal unity   exploitation   remind
    confidence.

Jesus as our High Priest

Although Jesus was never a priest nor did He ever pass any priestly examinations, He is described in the New Testament book of Hebrews as the Christians' 'High Priest' for ever. He is the One who came to act as a mediator or 'go-between', between God and man. He explained what God wanted from man and He acted as man's perfect sacrifice. He made it possible for man to approach God directly because He is man's representative and He presents everyone to God as they are—but with their faults forgiven by Him.

TASK G

1 Look for the New Testament book called Hebrews. Read the following references: *Hebrews 5: v 1–10; 9: v 1–15.*
2 In what way do they explain what has been said in this last section about Jesus?
3 Act one of the passages or stories in this unit.

28 A temple in Bali

36

IDEAS TO DEVELOP
Art
Paint a picture of the scene in *1 Kings 18: v 20–40.*

Charts
Make a chart to show how the idea of a priest evolved.

Cut five circles of white paper each with a radius of 8 cm. Paint or draw the five stages and stick them on a sheet of black sugar paper. Here are the stages in a jumbled order.

Temple sacrifices	Cure sickness
Spiritual interpreter	Help crops to grow
National leaders	

Diagram
Use a double page of your work book and make a series of six small diagrams to show the kind of work holy men performed as explained in this unit.

Living Language
1 Write six sentences to show the meaning of these words:

endure	roam	mediator
interpreter	inflated	haemorrhage

2 Priests, like other people who are specialists, have their own special types of clothing and special ways of talking.

If you heard the following speeches, could you tell what the speaker did for a living?

a 'If I had not missed the penalty we should have won.'

b 'If the going is dry Monarch is sure to do well.'

c 'Hand me some copper piping and look for the soldering'.

Can you make up some of your own to test on your friends?

3 Who do you think uses:

busby	boots	belt
cold store	knives	large mincer
hook	net	engine

Can you make up some others to test on your friends?

Do you think it was a good thing for priests to wear uniforms?

4 Some holy men tried to foretell the future by reading the stars. Collect as many horoscopes as you can from different newspapers and magazines for the same week. Put them all side by side. How similar or different are they? Put these down in column form in your class books.

5 Are horoscopes valuable? Discuss.

Deductive Work
Why would it have been a bad idea to have all the tribal priests in one family?

(*Clue:* young   death   sudden   plague successors)

Library Work

1   Find out what you can about the symptoms, effect and cures
of leprosy in the Bible:
Look up the following chapters:
Leviticus 13, 14 and 15.
There is a famous story about Naaman the Syrian in *2 Kings 5*.
Can you find any more?

2   Father Damien was the first to give his life to a leper colony.
Find out all you can about this person and the result of his work.

Bible Research

1   How did one Old Testament holy man help a lady? *1 Sam. 1:
v 9–18*.

2   A very important holy man in the New Testament was John the
Baptist.
Read *Luke 3: v 1–20;* and *Matt. 3: v 1–17*.
  a   What did he wear?
  b   What did he eat?
  c   What did he tell the priests to do?
  d   What did he tell ordinary people to do?
  e   What did he tell the publicans or tax collectors to do?
  f   What did he tell the soldiers to do?
  g   What did he do to Jesus?

3   The Pharisees (or strict Jewish teachers) wanted Jesus to
prove that he was a holy man by giving them a sign.
Read *Mark 8: v 11–13* and *Matthew 16: v 1–3*.
  a   What did he say?
  b   What did Jesus mean?
  c   Has this any meaning for us today?

Further Research

From the churches in your area find out what kind of work the
'priest' does. Write out your work under the heading of:
  a   Worship.
  b   Visiting.
  c   Welfare Work.

Discussion

1   In Unit 1 Jesus was described as the Great Healer. He insisted
that the person was only healed because of his faith in God.
'Belief in the doctor is more important than the medicine.'
Discuss.

2   Have holy men in the past done a worth-while job? Does the
priest have a future in our society?

3   What kind of person do you think is likely to become a holy
man?

Unit 4
Gifts to Gods

The two armies were locked together in mortal combat. But the battle was strange because these ferocious fighters instead of killing one another tried to knock their enemy out, rope him up and carry him away to their homes. This always happened when the Aztecs fought against surrounding nations, because the armies wanted to sacrifice their prisoners to their victorious war god rather than kill them on the battlefield. It was a blood chilling way of thanking their war god. Some say that as many as 20,000 prisoners were sacrificed by the Aztecs in one day as a victory celebration.

We have seen that as people settled down in communities with each man working at his trade, it was necessary to have special holy men. The holy man learnt certain actions which he hoped, when performed, would result in winning the favour of the gods. No one knows when man first felt a sense of sin. However, people could not help wondering sometimes whether they had upset the gods and, if so, whether these gods would punish them by sending them either disease or defeat in battle or even death. So they believed that the only way to rid themselves of this feeling of guilt or to avoid any likely punishment by the gods was to offer them gifts in the form of sacrifices.

29 Aztec priests prepare prisoners for sacrifice

TASK A

1 Try to think of some of the first things you did wrong at home or at school. How did you feel at the time? How did you try to get rid of your feeling of guilt?

2 Look up the story of David meeting Nathan, the prophet, in *2 Samuel 11: v 2 to 12: v 15.* What terrible sin did he commit? How did Nathan convince him of it? What did David do afterwards?

The people not only offered sacrifices to the gods to avoid punishment and to ask forgiveness for their wrong doing, but they also sacrificed to make certain that their crops would grow and sometimes to make sure of victory in battle. Sacrifices were therefore made to win either personal forgiveness or favour in battle or food for the tribe.

TASK B

1 Many people have had to make sacrifices. Consider the following people. What kind of sacrifices do you think they would have to make in life and what kind of needs would they have?

   a A mother.

   b An army officer.

   c A member of the royal family.

   d A famous pop star.

   e Any others you can think of.

2 Abraham left Haran to go to an unknown land because he felt God called him to go. What kind of sacrifice do you think this involved? Read the story once more in *Genesis 12: v 1–8* to refresh your memories.

30

Sacrifice amongst the Early Tribes

Many of these sacrifices amongst early tribes seem cruel by modern standards. But in many of these early communities sacrifices were done for the best and highest possible motive.

The people only sacrificed the <u>best</u> of their most valued possessions—either a first born son or a fine bullock or a spotless sheep. The poor people offered less costly animals.

The Priests and Sacrifice

The priest's main duty was to inspect sacrifices closely to see if they were without blemish, in order to make them acceptable to the gods.

30 Objects of sacrifice: warriors sacrificed to the sea–Saxons; coconuts–Pacific Islanders; seal–Eskimos; fruits–Indians; rice–Japanese

31 The Sioux buffalo feast

1   Here are some examples of sacrifices performed by various tribes in an effort to try to persuade the gods to provide them with more food.

The Sioux Indians held a great feast in honour of their god WAKAN TANKA at the end of the buffalo-hunting season. By so doing they hoped that their gods would make the buffalo plentiful for them during the next season.

Similarly Eskimos held autumn feasts in honour of the goddess SEDNA, whom they thought lived under the ice, asking her to provide them with fish and seals throughout the long, dark and icy winter.

31

2   Secondly, as has been said, sacrifices were sometimes performed to try to win forgiveness from the gods.

The Balinese thought it was sinful for children to fight. If any were caught fighting they would, as we say, 'be sent to Coventry' by the tribe for fifty days. If during that time they spoke or were spoken to, they had to pay a fine in the form of a sacrifice.

The Eskimos believed that when anyone sinned an unseen cloud formed over their heads. Only the goddess SEDNA, the ANGACUT or priest, and certain animals such as the caribou could see it. The only way to remove this dreadful cloud which hung over the tribe's head was for the person concerned to admit to everybody that he had sinned. What made matters worse was the belief that unless that person admitted his sin the caribou would not allow itself to be caught whilst the cloud hung over the sinner's head.

3   Lastly, sacrifices were offered either to win the god's favour or simply as a gesture of thanks.

The Maya Indians dedicated themselves to their many gods by making 'blood' sacrifices. They pushed a thorn through their tongues and the blood was placed on the altar as a living sacrifice.

Similarly, the Pah Utes Red Indians tore their ears with thorns, bathed in icy water and starved themselves, in an effort to persuade the Great Spirit to show his favour by giving them a vision and providing a guardian spirit to watch over them.

TASK C

1   What do you think, from what you have read, was the main single reason for offering sacrifices?

2   Why did so many sacrifices include blood as the most important part?

The Giving of Life

Since Holy Men or Priests, on the one hand, were thought of as God's representatives, on the other hand the sacrificed victim (whether animal or human) was given on behalf of the individual or tribe. The victim was their representative. The worshipper was showing in a SYMBOLIC way that he was willing to offer his own life to the gods.

Hebrew Sacrifices

The Hebrews sacrificed animals and the blood was collected carefully into a bowl. One half of the blood would be sprinkled over the worshippers, the other half would be burnt on the altar. In this way the person performing the sacrifice thought he was giving his life to God. The spilt blood was the animal's life 'essence' and as the animal's throat was slit and the blood carefully collected, so its life was being drained away. To many of these early tribes blood meant life and to spill blood was to sacrifice life. So in offering sacrifices the Hebrews were dedicating their own lives to God by way of the animal substitute. They rarely killed themselves, since Abraham had realised that his God Yahweh did not want human sacrifices when he had almost killed his own son Isaac, on an altar on Mount Moriah. Consequently, the Hebrews did the next best thing and offered the choicest of their own livestock.

This idea of a 'substitute' is seen more clearly in the Hebrew custom of choosing a particular goat by lot. On a special day called the DAY OF ATONEMENT, a goat would be driven away into the desert to die. The word ATONEMENT means 'covering' so during this day the sins of all the Nation were thought to have been covered over by God. This special goat was in effect the SCAPEGOAT and all the sins of the people were symbolically placed on the goat and offered to God. In this way the Hebrews hoped to obtain forgiveness.

32 Eskimo sprinkling blood
33 The sacred four-horned altar

32

Altars

Altars were places on which sacrifices were offered.

It seems that from the earliest days man everywhere felt the need for an altar. An altar was simply a holy spot. It was considered to be 'Holy' because of something strange that had happened there: a vivid dream or vision; a memorable victorious battle; a startling miracle; or it was simply a spot where a famous person had died.

TASK D

What happened at the places where the following people set up altars?

Abraham   *Gen. 13.*
Jacob   *Gen. 28: v 10–17 and 35: v 6–7.*
Moses   *Exodus 17: v 8–16.*
Saul   *1 Sam. 14: v 31–35.*

34

Early Altars

35

Whilst man was still a hunter, animal meat and fruit were so scarce that he rarely offered proper sacrifices. The hunter simply left the skull and bones, antlers or horns of the beast on the altar.

In the Caucasian Mountains, many such bones were discovered in natural caves. Sometimes the walls of these caves were covered with paintings of their favourite animals which hunters hoped their gods would help them catch.

The SAMOYEDE tribe of North America hunted the reindeer and when they had made a kill they mounted the skull and main bones on a rectangular board. This was fixed to a pole and driven into the ground. This pole was their TOTEM or emblem and the reindeer was regarded as their sacred animal.

Altars were often simply mounds of earth or piles of stones or caves. Most altars were usually situated on hills or high slopes. This is why they were sometimes called HIGH PLACES. It was not until people settled down and built permanent temples and churches that they could afford to build beautiful altars.

TASK E

1   Why were altars built on hill tops? (*Clue:* nearer.)
2   Look up these two references and explain what happened at the places mentioned:
    Jeremiah 32: v 35 (v 26–41)
    Leviticus 26: v 30 (v 27–33)
3   Where did Jesus go to pray? Read *Matthew 14: v 23; Matthew 26: v 30, 36–46.*
    Why do you think He chose such a spot?

What Was Sacrificed on these Altars?

Normally worshippers wanted to show their own personal devotion by offering something to the gods. This they did by offering their most choice possessions.

The TAHITIANS of Polynesia thought that the main part of life was in the stomach. Therefore when they made a kill they removed all of the internal organs most carefully and placed them on their altars.

An Odd Custom

The Eskimos of North America did not consider that the bones or entrails were as important as the brain and marrow — which is the content of the bone. When they made a kill they removed the brain from the skull and the marrow from the bones and submerged both in water which was free from fish. This was their offering or sacrifice to their underwater goddess, Sedna. They did it hoping that it would bring them good luck in future hunting expeditions.

Reindeer hunters sometimes took the carcass to a shaman who cut open the reindeer's chest and stomach, placed stones in the stomach, sewed everything up again and submerged the animal in a nearby lake as a sacrifice.

In these crude but costly ways early man showed his devotion to his gods. His was a simple form of worship, but he sincerely thought that the gods were worthy of the best animal or food sacrifice he could provide.

34 Cave paintings
35 A Samoyede totem
36 Sacrifice of reindeer

36

Human Sacrifices

The greatest possible sacrifice a person could make was either himself or his child.

The AZTECS were obsessed by human sacrifices and some maintain that at least 2,500 of their own people were sacrificed every year. Most of these victims had volunteered because they thought that in this way they could win everlasting life. These victims were often treated like gods. After they had been killed they were skinned and the priests dressed themselves up in these human skins. The crowds often shared in the sacrifice by eating part of the flesh. The heart was never eaten but was offered up to the gods. By doing this the people hoped that part of the god's spirit would enter into them.

In a slightly similar way the PAWNEE INDIANS sacrificed their most beautiful maiden at the ceremony of the Morning Star. Her heart was also offered separately to the Great Spirit. Only the best was good enough!

The CHALDAEANS, more generally known as the Babylonians, were known to have sacrificed human beings during their New Year festival in honour of their moon goddess, called SIN. This festival took place in their temple called a ZIGGURAT or pinnacle. (The moon god was called Nannar.) At one time they also sacrificed the first born child of the family.

The CANAANITES, who are so often mentioned in the Bible, sacrificed not only animals but young children of eight to ten years to their own BAALIM gods.

The HEBREWS, from the days of Abraham, as has been said before, believed that it was wrong to sacrifice human beings to God. Abraham realised this when God prevented him from sacrificing his son Isaac on Mount Moriah and instead provided him with a ram that had been caught in a thicket. However, at times even some of the Hebrews yielded to this temptation and sacrificed children and human beings to their God.

37 A ziggurat

TASK F

1 Read this story of the near sacrifice of Isaac on Mount Moriah: *Genesis 22: v 1–18*.

2 One famous person who did evil in the sight of God was Manasseh. Read *2 Kings 21: v 1–9*. Make a careful list of his sins and see how they fit in with what you have read in this book so far.

3 Do you think the tribes mentioned above were people who were completely evil and cruel?

The Four Main Kinds of Hebrew Sacrifices

The Hebrews had two main kinds of offerings: animals, and crops or fruit. The animals sacrificed were usually bullocks or oxen, sheep and lambs, goats and kids, or, if a person were very poor, doves and pigeons. The meal offerings were wheat, corn, barley, wine or UNLEAVENED bread.

The four types of sacrifices were:

a The Burnt Offering *See Levit. 22: v 17–20;* or *Numbers 15: v 1–13.*

b The Peace Offering *Levit. 3: v 1–17.*

c The Sin Offering *Levit. 4: v 1–5 and 13.*

d The Guilt Offering *Levit. 5: v 14–19; 7: v 1–7.*

Even though these sacrifices may seem strange to us it must be remembered that the outward form of the sacrifice was not as important as its inner or spiritual meaning.

a The burnt offering was given to show a person's devotion to God. It always showed the person's willingness to do God's will.

b The peace offering was a simple expression of thanks to God for His blessings.

c The sin offering was public confession of sin and it showed, in a symbolic way, that the person sacrificing was determined to do better in future.

d Lastly, the guilt offering was a special additional sacrifice for a terrible sin. During this sacrifice part of the animal would be waved before the altar supposedly to make the person sacrificing feel that his sins had been waved away. In this way he would be given the opportunity to experience forgiveness.

TASK G

What do you consider were the main differences between Jewish sacrifices and others mentioned in this chapter?

Jesus as God's Gift to Man

Look carefully at the above title again. This provides a clue to the understanding of the belief Christians hold about Jesus. So far in this chapter we have seen how many different peoples have tried to please their gods. Many tried either to win the god's favour or expressed simple thanks to the gods by offering the best possible sacrifice. The Christian, however, believes that the true God has shown His love and concern for man's welfare by sending and sacrificing Himself in and through a historical person called Jesus of Nazareth. All that God demands from Christians from now on is that they should accept Jesus and that they should sacrifice themselves—their time, talents and abilities in the service of others, as He did before them.

IDEAS TO DEVELOP

Art and Craft

1 Make a cloth picture of any one sacrifice mentioned in this chapter.

   a Collect as many odd scraps of different coloured cloths as you can.

   b Draw the picture and cut suitable pieces of cloth into the correct shapes and stick them on the drawing—odd pieces of fur look attractive.

   c Paint in the background with bold colours.

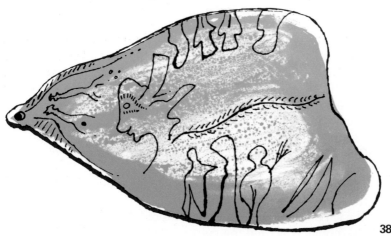

38

38 A bone pendant
39 Four Hebrew sacrificial offerings

   This early bone pendant is over 10,000 years old and was discovered in a cave in Raymondon, France. It shows a bison's head with the spine and several legs on either side. There are four human beings above and three below the head. One of them is carrying a palm leaf and on his right are objects that look like bows. This pendant would be worn around the neck like a lucky charm.

2 Design your own pendant to show:

   Either

      Sacrifices of war,

   Or

      Sacrifices made in the home.
      Make your own model in card first.

Charts

This chapter has shown that there is a chain of six events in most religions which ordinary people have used to try to approach God. Draw these six events on circles of art paper which have a radius of 8 cm. Link the circles together with 2 cm wide strips of black sugar paper.

Diagrams

Divide each side of a double page into quarters. On one page draw in two of the quarters two Jewish sacrifices and in the adjoining two quarters describe these sacrifices. On the facing page draw and describe the other two Jewish sacrifices.

Living Language

1 Write six sentences to show that you know the meaning of these words:

symbolic	ferocious	mortal
gesture	conscience	devotion.

2 Write six sentences under the title 'Why Sacrifice?' Here are some key words:

a	curry	favour	spirits	
b	feed	keep	gods	alive
c	God	create	life	return
d	gift	gratitude	mercy	
e	bribe	gods	help	fight
f	gain	forgiveness	sins	

3 Ask as many people as possible in school and elsewhere what they mean by the word 'sacrifice'. Write their replies down and compare them with the replies received by others in the class. Make a short play to show these different meanings of the word 'sacrifice'.

Deductive Work

1 Before the Anglo-Saxon seafaring warriors became Christians they were willing to sacrifice human beings to their gods after making journeys in their ships.
What two things did they sometimes sacrifice?
(*Jumbled clues:* fiehcs   rrawsroi   sbtao)

2 The Anglo-Saxons were seafaring pirates before they settled down in Britain. On occasions they used to throw ten prisoners into the sea. Why? (*Jumbled clue:* cefiriacs   aes   ogd)

3 In a hospital chapel at Nazareth the altar is a carpenter's bench. Why do you think this should be so appropriate?

Puzzles

Make up a quiz that includes the following words:

prisoners	Bali
Nathan	blood
spotless	desert
Sioux	reindeer
Angacut	marrow

Library Work

These three famous people sacrificed themselves for others:
Joan of Arc.
Polycarp.
Granville Sharp.
Who were they?
What did they do?
What effect did they have?

Bible Research

1 Find out what the Bible says about the following questions:
   a What should the Hebrews sacrifice? *Read Leviticus 1*.
   b How were they to react? *Psalm 4: v 5; Psalm 107: v 22; Psalm 27: v 6; Psalm 51: v 17; Hebrews 10: v 19–24; 26–31*.
   c What is the effect of a sacrifice? *Proverbs 15: v 8; Proverbs 21: v 3; Isaiah 1: v 11–20*.
   d What do these verses tell you about the Hebrew attitude towards sacrifices? Discuss this attitude amongst yourselves.

2 What does the Bible say about altars?
   The following men built altars to God:
   a Noah in *Genesis 8: v 20–22*.
   b Abram in *Genesis 22: v 9–14*.
   c Moses in *Exodus 17: v 13–16*.
   d Joshua in *Joshua 8: v 14–32*.
   e Gideon in *Judges 6: v 14–32*.
   In each case find out:
   a the reason for building the altar.
   b where the altars were placed.
   If you are interested in the subject of altars use a modern Bible dictionary and trace all the references you can find to altars in the Bible.

Further Research

1 a Go out to the local churches in your area and find out what different kinds of altars there are to be found in churches of different denominations.
      Draw pictures of:
      The different fonts,
      The different altars.
   b If there are no altars try to discover why that particular church has none.
2 What is put on an altar in a church?
3 What other objects do you find in a church and what are they used for?

Discussion

1 What is the greatest sacrifice you could reasonably be expected to make for:
   your school,
   your family,
   your faith?
2 One has heard of Buddhists burning themselves to death for their beliefs but many Christians would say that God wants living human sacrifices, not dead ones. Discuss.

Unit 5
A Programme of Life

Almost every family owns a photograph album which is taken out occasionally to show friends or to remind older people of past events and memories.

This picture shows a family group covering four generations, but this family, like all families, can be traced back much further than that. Our present Royal Family is called Mountbatten-Windsor and its family line can be traced back to the days of William the Conqueror (A.D. 1066), perhaps even further to a Saxon King called Egbert (A.D. 802).

41 Four generations

TASK A

1 Draw your family tree to show, if possible, the last six generations.

2 Try to follow the family tree in your father's or mother's family back as far as possible.

3 a *Genesis 11: v 10–32.*
   Whose family tree is this?

  b *Exodus 6: v 14–27.*
   Whose tribal genealogy is this?

  c What is the main difference between Jesus's two family trees in *Matthew 1: v 1–17* and *Luke 3: v 23–38?*

  (*Clue:* To whom are they traced back?)

If your family has an album it probably shows pictures, mostly of babies, of marriages, and of grandparents some of whom are now dead. In this way we can see how life's programme usually contains the three major events of birth, marriage and death. The first two usually bring great joy but the last generally brings sorrow. But even with this last event in life, many people have always had an idea that death is not really the end.

The First Part
of Life's Programme Is Birth

42

Babies have always been treated as a source of great blessing. The mystery of birth has produced some strange beliefs among most tribes.

The Eskimos believed that every person had two souls. When a person died, one soul went to a new life elsewhere while the other soul stayed near the dead body until another baby was born. This soul then entered the new baby as its 'guardian' spirit.

Similarly, the Sherpa tribesman of the Himalayas, who are Buddhists, tried to solve the strange mystery of birth and death by saying that a baby's life was due to the rebirth of a dead person.

Normally the birth of a baby has always been regarded as a blessing so the Yoruba of Nigeria naturally thought that the birth of twins would be a double blessing. But their neighbours, the Ibo, thought that the birth of twins was an evil sign and they put twins in the jungle to be eaten by wild animals.

42 An Ibo destroys the evil sign
43 Can they survive?

Wherever man had great difficulty in finding or growing enough food, the birth of a baby was often a sad event. Because food was so scarce in some parts of the world, new born babies had to be killed mercifully to avoid a slow death by starvation. The Aborigines of the scorching Australian desert and the Eskimos of the ice region both faced this problem of scarcity of food by mercy killing. The Eskimo, however, thought that when they deliberately killed a child its soul went straight to Heaven.

43

The Holy Man and Birth

Babies were nearly always taken to the holy man to be blessed in some way. For instance, the Navaho Indian mothers had newly born babies baptised by the holy man who sprinkled corn pollen over their heads. Each mother then bathed her baby and finally wrapped it in cotton cloth.

Birth in the Bible

The birth of a boy to the Hebrews was a far greater source of joy than the birth of a girl. When a boy was born, the whole village, as well as the parents, were joyous. The village musicians would play their instruments and everywhere people would be dancing. But in the case of the birth of a girl there was very little rejoicing.

A Hebrew boy was taken to the Temple at Jerusalem when he was only eight days old to be given a name and made acceptable to God.

TASK B

What happened to Jesus when He was eight days old? *Read Luke 2: v 21—40.*

The First-born Hebrew Boy

A first-born Hebrew boy was considered to be sacred to God and parents had to buy him back from God by paying the priests five shekels (about £0·75 in our money).

Look up this custom in *Numbers 18: v 16*. But the money used to buy the first-born back could not be paid by the parents until the child was thirty-one days old.

It was also a Jewish custom to allow the first-born to inherit twice as much as other sons. *See 1 Kings 2: v 9; Luke 15: v 11–32; 2 Chronicles 21: v 1–3.*

Another highlight in a Hebrew boy's early life was when he became a 'Son of the Law'. From that time on he was considered to be a confirmed member of the Jewish faith. This event normally occurred at the age of twelve. He would have to visit the temple in Jerusalem where the priest explained to him how he was responsible for keeping the Law and in particular the Ten Commandments. *See Exodus 20: v 1–17.*

TASK C

1 Why do you think the birth of a boy was usually welcomed by most people?
2 Why did the eldest son receive twice as much of the father's property? (*Clue:* chieftain, *Genesis 49: v 3; Deuteronomy 21: v 17.*)
3 What happened to Jesus when He was twelve years old? *Luke 2: v 42–52.*
4 'Boys are stronger than girls and are far more important.' Discuss.

44 Till death us do part

The Second Highlight in the Programme of Life Is Marriage

All animals possess a 'mating instinct', which is necessary to produce young. Some animals, like cheetahs, are known to keep one mate for life but this is not usual among animals. However, people today generally have only one husband or wife.

Nevertheless, it is quite a modern idea for a person to be allowed to marry someone with whom he or she falls in love. Formerly it was much more usual to have marriages 'arranged'. Even today, for instance, the Masai tribesmen of East Africa have 'arranged' marriages. The fathers arrange for the boy and girl to be married and for the husband's family to give the wife's family a gift or dowry.

Throughout the world it has not been unusual in the past for men to have more than one wife, especially if the wives did the work! In a few places where warriors were needed and the food supply was short it was known for each woman to have several husbands.

In Southern India, the Toda tribesmen deliberately killed baby girls at birth in order to produce a shortage of women.

In the Old Testament we read that many famous Hebrew men had more than one wife. But the Hebrews gradually came to realise that human life could only be fully respected when one man had one wife.

It was not usual for Hebrew 'newly weds' to go away for a honeymoon or holiday, but instead they stayed at home and kept an open house. They dressed up in their best suits and everyone in the village treated them like royalty.

Even amongst the Hebrews the choice of a wife was usually left to the young man's parents. But often young men were allowed to choose their brides, and on rare occasions young women chose their own husbands. Once a match had been made there was an exchange of presents. This present or DOWRY could be made in the form of servants or property, or by working for a certain length of time.

The wedding ceremony took place in a Jewish building, called a SYNAGOGUE. It was very similar to our present church ceremony. However, one strange Hebrew custom was for the husband or the relatives to cover the bride with a cloak. It was to show that the wife would be protected by the husband for the rest of her life. The wedding guests offered blessings (*Genesis 24: v 60*) and the bride's father drew up a marriage contract.

TASK D

1 Read the story of Jacob's marriage in Genesis 29. How did he pay for a dowry? How was he swindled?
2 King Solomon is said to have had more than one wife. Find out how many he had from *1 Kings 11: v 6–13*.
3 What happened when Jesus went to a wedding? *John 2: v 1–10*.
4 How much wine did he make? (1 firkin is about 41 litres.)

The Third Stage in the Programme of Life Is Death

The last and final item in everyone's programme of life is death. This is still the greatest mystery of all. Death was understood in the past as either a natural event or the result of an evil power.

First of all death was thought of by some simply as a continuation of life. The dead person lived on in the other world exactly as he had left the present one. So the Sioux warriors had no fear of dying in battle because they believed that if they died whilst they were still young they would remain young forever in the spirit world. But if any Sioux grew old and weak, he would be old and incapable in the future life.

The EGYPTIANS often thought of death as a natural thing and took great care to prepare the dead person for a long journey. Since it was thought to be similar to the present life, it was necessary to give the corpse plenty of food and important people such as the Pharaohs even had their wives, servants, pet animals and treasured possessions buried with them. Some of these Pharaohs are buried in what are now recognised to be the greatest tombs of all time – the Pyramids.

The VIKINGS did a similar thing when their kings died. Dead slaves, weapons, food and even horses were put into a ship which would be launched to drift unsteered, or be burnt or buried.

45

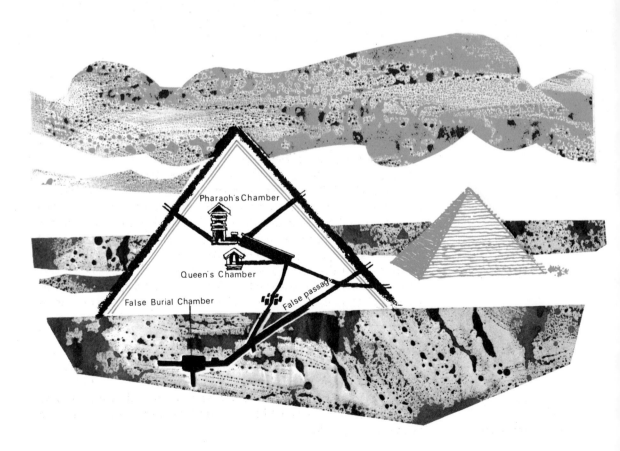

Pharaoh's Chamber

Queen's Chamber

False Burial Chamber

False passage

46

TASK E

At one time the Anglo-Saxons buried their kings like the Vikings. One of their burial ships was dug up at Sutton Hoo. Read about it in a book about the Anglo-Saxons (*Dewey* 942.01) and make a drawing of it on a double page in your work book.

Other people thought that life was quite different after death. The INCAS of Peru dressed themselves in black when one of them died. If the person who had died had been famous, official mourning for him could last for a whole year. The Incas placed the corpse in a sitting position, with all its belongings by its side and afterwards everything would be burnt. At first it was customary for them, as with the Pharaohs, to burn the famous dead Inca's servants and slaves at the same time. The Incas' view of death was an ANIMISTIC one. That is, they believed that the dead person's spirit lived on in animals, plants or on distant mountains. Therefore they showed the greatest respect for animals and they believed that if they failed to do so the animal's 'spirit' would prevent them from catching more of that kind of animal in future. The Incas also believed that if a dead person had been good then he would go to live near the sun and enjoy warmth and good food. But if an Inca had been wicked he would be sent under the earth to eat pebbles in the gloomy cold.

45 An Egyptian Pharaoh's tomb

46 A Viking burial ship

Not all primitive people accepted the possibility of life after death. For instance, the Masai herders did not believe in an after life. They exposed their dead to jackals and other animals of prey. However, even though they did not believe in any after-life, they still placed the corpse in such a position that it would be ready to go on a journey, if it were necessary, with plenty of food and other provisions placed alongside the corpse.

TASK F

1 If we had the same beliefs as ancient and primitive people, what kind of objects do you think we would bury alongside a dead person today?

2 a 'Don't save up—you cannot take it with you.' Discuss.
  b Jesus said something similar in the story of the Rich Fool. Write down this story in your own words placing it in a modern setting. *(Luke 12: v 13–21.)*

The Hebrew View of Death

The Hebrew had a very simple belief about death. After a person died the Hebrews thought his spirit went to a shadowy world called SHEOL.

The most popular and common belief of the Hebrews about the after life was the one which suggested that dead people lived in another world where they could remember the past and see future events. They could return to this earth to the place where they had lived. The ancient Hebrews also left food and supplies by the side of the corpse. The 'other life' is described in the Old Testament either as:

1 A place where other people had gathered from the past.
2 A place of the fathers.
3 A place where one 'sleeps' with other members of the family.

The Hebrews were convinced that in the other world friends, relatives and lovers could recognise each other. It is not clear where they thought this world was, it could be in Sheol or in the family grave. Much later, many Jewish religious leaders became convinced that the other world was a place where God prepared man for even greater glory.

The Christians, who accepted that Jesus was the Messiah, were convinced at first that they would die and stay in the other world until Jesus came again a second time. This was the Last Day or Judgment Day when all who had died would rise again from the tombs and be judged by the God of the dead and the living.

It was therefore unthinkable for a Hebrew to be cremated. Instead, he was carefully washed, rubbed with oils and spices and wrapped in a linen cloth, with a napkin placed over the head. The body was then put either in a grave or a natural cave.

TASK G

One of the most famous people in the Old Testament is said to have never died!

1 Read the story of this person in *2 Kings 2: v 9–14.*   47

2   What do you think really happened to him?

3   When did the Hebrews believe he would return to earth? *Malachi 4: v 5; Matthew 11: v 14.*

Jesus and Death

Jesus did not want to die. In fact He went through great anxiety of mind and asked God not to make Him carry on with the crucifixion. See *Matthew 26: v 37–39.* Throughout His life He had loved and helped the sick and the needy – He had even raised Lazarus from the dead. There was so much left to do and He was naturally tempted to ask Himself: why die? However, He was convinced that the love in Him was the love of God the Father, and that the Father would raise Him from the dead just as surely as the power of His love had succeeded in raising His friend Lazarus.

TASK H

1   When Jesus rose from the dead everybody was shocked beyond words. Some claim that His disciples only saw a ghost, but what does *Luke 24: v 31–44* tell you Jesus thought about that idea?

2   'Seeing is believing'. Is this always true? Make a list of all the different things you believe in and yet cannot see.

48   **IDEAS TO DEVELOP**
Art and Craft

Make a rubbing of a Viking funeral ship. You can read about it on page 41 of *Finding Out About the Vikings* by D. Philips-Birt, *Dewey* 948.

a   Draw a sideview picture of a Viking ship on a piece of card and cut it out. Do not let it be less than 20 cm long.

b   Key lines can be drawn on the ship with heavy ball point lines.

c   Stick pieces of paper on the ship to show important things such as shields, oars, etc.

d   Put a thin piece of white paper over the card picture. Rub all over it with the side of dark wax crayons. Watch the picture come out on the paper. Try it out several times with different pieces of paper and different coloured crayons.

e   If you mix the colours it will look even better.

Charts

Many people in the world such as the Australian aborigines believe that dead people are reborn in babies. Draw this chart of life as they understand it.

Draw pictures in each quadrant (i.e. a quarter of a circle). The circle should have a radius of at least 15 cm.

49 Plan for a chart
50 The Entombed Christ

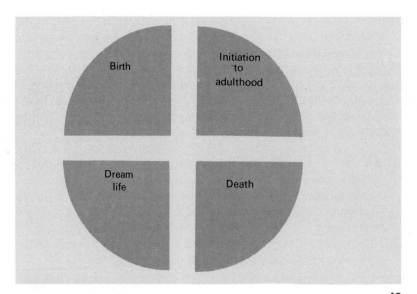

49

Diagrams

Make a good clear diagram of your family tree from either your mother's or your father's side, going back six generations if possible.

Living Language

1 Write six sentences to show that you know the meaning of these words.

generations   genealogy   guardian
programme   scorching   inherited

2 Here are eight sentences about birth amongst the Australian aborigines. Write out the sentences in their correct order.

  a The baby is covered with grease and ashes to protect it from the sun.
  b The women and baby catch up the rest of the tribe at night-fall.
  c She digs a hollow in the sand.
  d The mother stops while the rest of the tribe walk on.
  e The mother marks a circle on the sand to keep the evil spirits away.
  f They march after the tribe whirling a lighted brand of fire around their heads to drive the evil spirits away.
  g The newborn baby which is a whitish colour is thought to come from the land of the spirits.
  h An older woman may stay to help her.

3 Act the story in *Luke 2: v 42–52.*

Deductive Work

Here is a picture entitled 'The Entombed Christ', which the Dutch artist Hans Holbein painted towards the middle of the sixteenth century. Why was Christ laid in a tomb?

Other people have disposed of bodies in different ways: how many different ways have been mentioned in this chapter? How many more can you discover? Find out how the Nootka Indians, the Assyrians, and the Tahitians disposed of their dead.

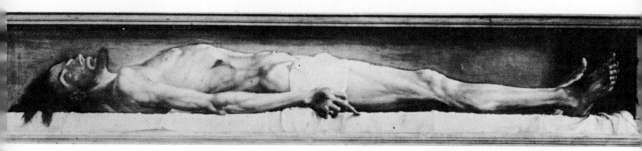

50

Puzzle

Here are six words. Look through the chapter and find which name or tribe is connected with each word:

corn pollen	rebirth	animistic
sheol	burial ship	jackals

Library Work

1 Make a study of Tutankhamen's tomb. (*Dewey* 932.)
   Find out:
   When it was opened.
   What was found.
   What happened to the men who opened it.
2 Find out all you can about the Viking belief about Valhalla. (*Dewey* 948·0).
3 Why is Somerset House in London so important?

Further Research

Ask six friends or relatives what they think happens after death.
Group all the class answers together under three headings:
a Life after death.
b Don't know.
c There is no life after death.
Discuss the results of your survey.

Discussion

Which is better—cremation or burial?

Unit 6
Under One Roof

51 Home

'It's eight o'clock Jim, time to get up for school. Your clean shirt is in your drawer; put a clean pair of socks on. Come on, hurry up or you will be late,' said his mother.

Jim arrives downstairs to see Mum fastening his sister's shoes and combing her hair.

Almost every person has experienced this sort of scene as he or she crawls out of bed and goes downstairs to join the rest of the family. As you walked past houses on your way to school you were probably walking past little groups of people who live as families and do a lot together. But not all families throughout the world are like our families. Where people live different kinds of lives they have different kinds of families, just as they have different foods and different religions. Pigmy hunters often have to split up their groups when there is a shortage of food, so the small family is most important to them. But the Masai warriors lived in much larger groups because they needed each other to form strong fighting bands. The Asanti farmers lived in large communities because they needed many people to till the land and manufacture food and goods. So an Asanti family included uncles, aunts and many other distant relatives.

TASK A

1   What is the difference between a family, a tribe and a nation?
2   Pair up these words correctly:
     family   tribe   country
     chieftain   government   parents
3   Put these words in what you consider to be an order of authority and explain briefly why you placed them in that order:
     judge   employer   parents   the Law
     the Prime Minister   police   the Queen's children

COLLOQUIALISM

FAITH, TRUST, CONFEDENCE

1) I have trust in my new car
2) I have perfect faith in my new car
3) I have great confedence in my new car.

2

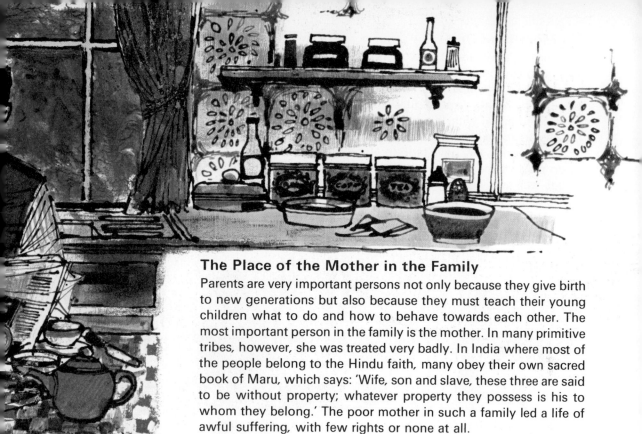

The Place of the Mother in the Family

Parents are very important persons not only because they give birth to new generations but also because they must teach their young children what to do and how to behave towards each other. The most important person in the family is the mother. In many primitive tribes, however, she was treated very badly. In India where most of the people belong to the Hindu faith, many obey their own sacred book of Maru, which says: 'Wife, son and slave, these three are said to be without property; whatever property they possess is his to whom they belong.' The poor mother in such a family led a life of awful suffering, with few rights or none at all.

Fortunately, other people, such as the Asanti, thought highly of their women because they traced back their family tree through the mother. It was the mother who actually gave birth to the children. Furthermore, since the Sherpas and Eskimos believed that the birth of a child gave the soul of a dead person the chance to live again, mothers were regarded as very important people.

One of the mother's chief tasks in every tribe was to teach her young children how to accept certain tribal customs. The Cheyenne Indians practised a Sun Dance once every year. To do this strings were fastened to a cottonwood tree that had been felled and stuck into the ground. The free ends were threaded through the flesh of the young braves' chests. They danced and danced until finally, after terrible suffering, the strings tore through their flesh and the braves felt that in this way they had pleased the Great Sun Spirit. From the earliest days they had been taught by their mothers to believe that this was a beautiful dance which was only performed by the best braves.

The mothers amongst the Boro Indians of the Amazon jungle grew the crops, and so enjoyed equality with the men because they controlled the food supply. A similar thing was clearly seen amongst some East African farmers where a woman was allowed to buy goods without her husband's consent, whereas a husband needed his wife's permission before he could borrow anything.

Jewish mothers were very important too and as teachers retold the early Hebrew stories to their children. Had they not done so the Old Testament stories which we read today and which were not written down for at least 1,200 years after Abraham's death would have been lost.

No More than One

Although a man in ancient days was allowed to have more than one wife normally only rich people could afford such luxury. A poor person could only afford to collect a dowry for one wife and she was usually highly respected by him. But she was not everywhere considered equal with the husband. He was still the head of the house and actually owned his wife.

A mother not only gave birth to numerous children but also had to do most of the manual work, such as fetching water from the village well and working in the fields.

If a husband took a second wife there was always the chance that the first wife would be neglected but she was usually treated very humanely.

52

TASK B

Look up the following verses in the Bible. (Use the Revised Standard Version.)

Exodus 2: v 2; Isaiah 66: v 2; Proverbs 1: v 8; Proverbs 19: v 26; Exodus 20: v 12; Proverbs 23: v 23; Ephesians 6: v 1.

Write these verses down in your class books. Put the most suitable word from the following list next to each verse.

humility	hide	honour	education
disobedience		listen	obey

The Father in the Family

Like most tribes the Hebrews have always thought that the head of a family should be the man. He could defend his family and he originally provided it with food by hunting. The mere fact that he was physically stronger than his wife emphasised his power.

The aborigines in Australia had tremendous power over their wives, but gradually over the centuries this has been lessening. Before Mohammed, the founder of the Islamic (or Moslem) religion, Arab women were little better treated than animals. Although he improved things slightly, it still took 1,500 years for Arab women to enjoy more freedom from their powerful husbands. Apart from this, Arab men were able to have three other wives as well.

52 Masai mother and child
53 The Hebrew father's tasks

The Hebrew Father

The Hebrews, however, tried to stop this happening by reminding men of their responsibilities to their wives and family. In ancient days a man was not only a father, a priest and a judge to his family but he was also responsible for teaching his trade to his sons. He also had to protect the family land from foreign invaders or greedy kings and nobles.

An unmarried Hebrew man had one strange responsibility. If his married brother died without leaving any children he had to marry the widow himself, so that she could give birth to children and continue the family name.

It was so important for a Hebrew man to have children that if his wife could not bear children he could make one of his slave women have a baby instead. There was a strange belief amongst the Hebrews that blessings (or sorrows) were passed on from father to son without end and it was therefore vital for a man to have at least one son.

TASK C

1   The Hebrews were allowed to marry foreigners until a priest named Ezra stopped it. Why do you think he did this? *Read Ezra 9: v 1–12.* (*Clues:* language, traditions and customs.)
2   Find out why a person today is not allowed to marry a near relative. Isaac and Jacob married relatives. Who were they? *Genesis 24: v 3–15, Genesis 28: v 1–4 and 29: v 16–30.*
3   How did Sarah talk to Abraham?
    Was Abraham her master or did she have powers over him? *Look up Genesis 18: v 9–15 and Genesis 21: v 1–21.*
4   Look up the following verses and write out, in your own words, what they say about Hebrew fathers:
    Exodus 15: v 2; Judges 17: v 10; Judges 18: v 18; 2 Samuel 10: v 2; Psalm 103: v 13; Proverbs 4: v 1; Job 29: v 16.
    Which of these verses tell you about a father's
    a   pity
    b   kindness
    c   teaching
    d   duty as a priest
    e   reaction to the poor.

Children in the Family

Today when news is passed around that Mrs. So-and-So is going to have a baby, women smile knowingly and everybody is quite excited, especially if it is the woman's first baby. The Health Service in Britain provides the mother-to-be with extra milk to safeguard the child. Once the child is born it is cared for very gently and well. Have you ever wondered how many hours of hard work a mother puts into looking after a child until it is old enough to look after itself? In spite of the parents' love for their children, they make themselves unpopular from time to time, by making clear demands on their offspring.

53

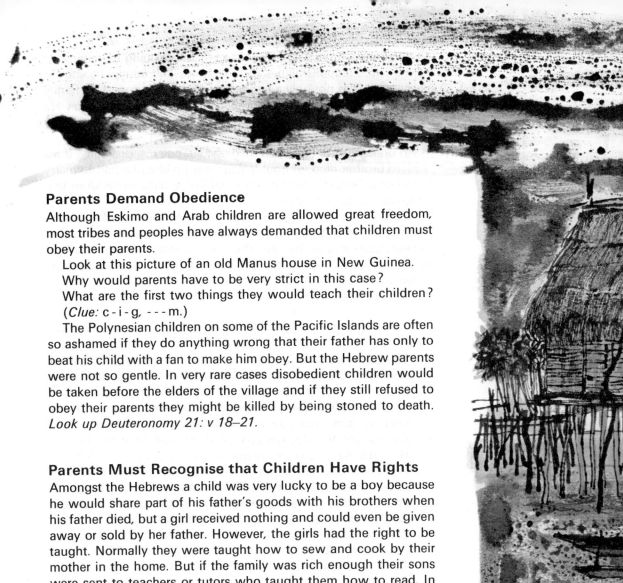

Parents Demand Obedience

Although Eskimo and Arab children are allowed great freedom, most tribes and peoples have always demanded that children must obey their parents.

Look at this picture of an old Manus house in New Guinea.

Why would parents have to be very strict in this case?

What are the first two things they would teach their children? (*Clue:* c - i - g, - - - m.)

The Polynesian children on some of the Pacific Islands are often so ashamed if they do anything wrong that their father has only to beat his child with a fan to make him obey. But the Hebrew parents were not so gentle. In very rare cases disobedient children would be taken before the elders of the village and if they still refused to obey their parents they might be killed by being stoned to death. *Look up Deuteronomy 21: v 18–21.*

Parents Must Recognise that Children Have Rights

Amongst the Hebrews a child was very lucky to be a boy because he would share part of his father's goods with his brothers when his father died, but a girl received nothing and could even be given away or sold by her father. However, the girls had the right to be taught. Normally they were taught how to sew and cook by their mother in the home. But if the family was rich enough their sons were sent to teachers or tutors who taught them how to read. In those days children usually learnt long passages out of the Old Testament by heart. Turn to *2 Samuel 1: v 17–27.* It is called David's Lament and is probably a typical passage which had to be learnt by Hebrew boys. It shows clearly how David felt when he heard of the death of Saul and Jonathan. Perhaps you could learn it in your spare time.

Parents Expect Children to Perform Duties

The father taught his sons a trade. When the father died the eldest son became the head of the family and he had to provide food and clothing for everybody else. This could be hard on him because Hebrew women had, on average, seven children in every family. So if a man had had more than one wife there would be quite a big family to look after! It is thought that Jesus had to look after his mother and brothers because his father Joseph probably died whilst Jesus was still a young man.

54 An old Manus house

TASK D

1 What other duties do you think a child should have towards his parents today? Make up your own list and compare your ideas with those of the rest of the form.
2 The Bible tries to explain how the various races of different colour and language came into existence. Read the story in *Genesis 11: v 1–9*. Draw in your class books your own design of the tower of Babel and in all the various sections put as many different races and their particular languages as you can remember. Compare your tower with those of the rest of the class.
3 Look up the following verses in the Bible and see what duties a Hebrew son had towards his family: *Exodus 20: v 12; Ephesians 6: v 1–3*.
4 Find out what kind of games Hebrew children played. Here are two books to help you.
   Everyday Life in Old Testament Times by E. W. Heaton (from page 91 onwards).
   Everyday Life in New Testament Times by A. C. Bouquet (from page 186 onwards).

The Hebrew Family

One of the most striking features of the Hebrew family, like those of the Aztecs and Incas, was the way that their religion was at the heart of everything they did. Look up these verses.
1 What was on the doorpost of the house? *Deut. 6: v 4–9 and 11: v 20*.
2 The chief commands of Yahweh were written in little boxes called PHYLACTERIES worn on the wrist and forehead. What were the commands in them? *Deut. 11: v 13–22*.
3 What did all the family do every week? Read *Luke 4: v 16*.
4 What happened if somebody hurt or killed a member of the family? *Exodus 21: v 23–25 and Leviticus 24: v 20*.

IDEAS TO DEVELOP
Art and Craft

EITHER

'Fashions change with the times.'
Try to find some old photographs of your great grandparents or grandparents and look carefully at the clothes they wore. Draw them on art paper on the left hand side of the page and opposite them compare them with the fashions of today.

OR

Modes of Transport.
In the past families were limited in their travel. Find some old photographs of the kind of transport used in your great grandparents' day. Draw them and compare them with similar transport today.

Make a model of your own house. In each appropriate room put a cut out picture of your parents, brothers and sisters and any object you can make which you have at home, e.g. a grandfather's clock.

Use two or more cardboard shoe boxes, one for the downstairs and one for the upstairs. Divide the box into as many rooms as you have at home.

Charts

On three large sheets of sugar paper build up charts to show what you believe to be the rights and responsibilities of:

mothers,
fathers,
children,

as shown in this project.

Choose your pictures and draw them on pieces of white paper 12 cm × 10 cm. Group them on your sugar paper neatly and label each sheet boldly.

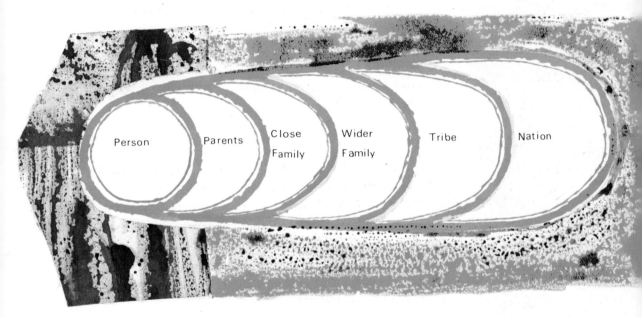

Person   Parents   Close Family   Wider Family   Tribe   Nation

The diagram above shows how each person is related to everyone else.

Draw a similar diagram in your class books replacing the above names by the names of your own family, neighbours and so on.

Living Language

1   Write down six sentences to show that you know the meaning of these words.

humane   pregnant   average
relatives   traditional   widow

2   What do these phrases mean?
   a   to smile knowingly
   b   enjoy equality with men
   c   the head of a family
   d   spare the rod and spoil the child

3 You should really do this at the end of the whole unit.

Gather together all the things you have learned about the family life of the Hebrews.

Make up a short play of a Hebrew family. Here are a few ideas to start you off.

Waking early	water		shepherd	boy
help	work	girl	mother	wash
stranger	hospitality		meal	prayer
news	brother killed		revenge	chase

OR Read the story of Abraham, Sarah and Hagar. *Genesis ch. 16: and 21.* Write a composition from either Abraham's or one of the women's point of view.

Deductive Work

1 At what time of the day would you fetch water if you were a Hebrew woman in Israel? (*Clue:* heat).

2 Read *John 4: v 4–26* (especially *v 6*). Why did this woman fetch her water at 12 o'clock? (The 6th hour means midday to the Jews.)

3 From this chapter can you work out six reasons why Christians call God 'Father'?

A Game

The ancient Hebrew stories were passed on orally (spoken).

To prove that stories change try this experiment.

a Choose a good story.

b Ask one person to record it on tape privately.

c One person only hears the story and whispers it to another person.

d This story is quietly passed from person to person.

e Ask the last child to record the story on tape.

f Play back the two stories and make a list of the differences.

56

Library Work

1 Find out what you can about any one of these three famous wives.

Elizabeth Fry.

Mrs. Pankhurst.

Madam Curie.

Find out:

a When they lived

b What they did

c What kind of difficulties they had to face

d What effect these had on their character

e One famous saying from each person

2 Find out what family life was like amongst one of these tribes:

The Aborigines

The Sioux Indians

55 Diagram of relationships
56 A Hebrew mother's tasks

Bible Research

1 Widows and orphans suffered greatly from poverty but the Bible laws were made to protect them. They would be provided for by the religious leaders and rich people. Look up these references and make out a list of the Jewish attitude towards widows and poor people: *Psalm 146: v 9; Job 29: v 12–16.* Compare these with: *Mark 12: v 38–40; Matthew 22: v 1–10; Acts 6: v 1–4.*

2 Jesus praised a widow on one occasion. Read the story in *Mark 12: v 42–44.* Why do you think she won Jesus's praise?

3 The short book of Ruth mentions one important topic in this project. Read *Ruth 2* to find out what it is.
Write out this story in the form of a play using your own words. Act it afterwards with two of your friends.

4 In what way did Jesus show He always had time for children? *Read Matthew 19: v 13–15.*

5 Jesus was the guest of Zacchaeus. Who was he? *Read Luke 19: v 1–9.* Why did the people protest?

Further Research

EITHER

Go to your local church and find out if there are any 'family' services held there and if so how they differ from the ordinary services.

OR

Try to find how much time a mother spends every day looking after a child at the ages of:

1 month
1 year
5 years
12 years

57

Discussion

1 Peter may have left his wife to follow Jesus. *Mark 1: v 16–18.* If so, was he right to do so?

2 What responsibilities do you think people have towards their parents?

3 If a complete stranger from abroad came to a British home what do you think would be its most striking single feature to him?

4 What effect would it have had on Israel if her great stories had been forgotten?

Unit 7

Speaking Without Words

What do we do more than anything else? Walk? Work? Talk? Read? Whatever you may decide, there is one thing we do which is obviously as important as anything else—that is using speech and language, because it is our method of communicating with each other. Although we depend upon words it is possible to 'talk' with signs instead. Here are six signs in deaf and dumb sign language.

Could you learn to 'talk' this way?

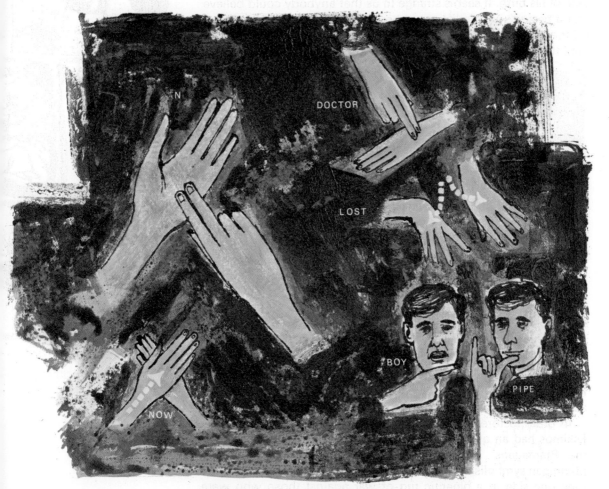

TASK A

What are the 26 most common signs we use? Think of other chief signs we use instead of words.

Religious Signs and Symbols

Throughout the world people have used signs and symbols in their religions. The most famous sign in many countries today is the Christians' Cross because it reminds people of the death of Jesus. There are, however, many different kinds of signs which have been and still are used to communicate different kinds of messages to other people.

Signs of Fear and Fate

Fortune tellers always fascinate us with their mysterious signs and their strange methods, and it all helps to provide an atmosphere of fascination and mystery.

The AZTECS divided time up into thirteen 'heavenly' signs. The Aztecs' soothsayers thought they could decide whether a newborn child was fit to be a priest, a warrior, an ordinary peasant or anything else simply by the sign which corresponded to the day and time of his birth. It seems strange to us that anybody could believe that a person's whole life could be set by the baby's birth sign. It is little wonder that parents and midwives never baptised children until there was a favourable birth sign for the baby.

Some signs served practical purposes and the ESKIMOS, for instance, learnt their signs quickly or they would not have been able to survive against their most cruel enemy—the bitter cold.

In order to foretell what the coming winter would be like the Eskimos had an autumn feast, called the Feast of the Ducks and the Ptarmigans. The duck symbolised the summer and the ptarmigan symbolised the winter. The Eskimos born in the summer took one side in a gigantic tug-of-war against those who were born in the winter. If the 'ducks' won, it was thought to be a sign that the winter would be mild but if the 'ptarmigans' won, it would be a hard winter.

AN INDIAN STORY

The most famous of the Sioux chiefs was Sitting Bull. He is said to have started the CULT of the Paradise bird. He claimed that this bird had saved his life at one time. He was only fourteen years old when he fell asleep under a tree. As he woke he saw a huge bear ambling towards him. Just as he was about to get up and run away he noticed a small bird above him in the tree. To his surprise the bird spoke and told him to lie still. The bear came up to him, sniffed his still body and turned away. The young boy immediately ran back to his camp singing and dancing with joy. The story of how he was helped by the bird spread and from that time onwards the paradise bird became a sign of protection from fear and a guide to every Sioux warrior.

TASK B

1 Some think that the Hebrews had two strange signs for knowing God's will:

a The Urim and the Thummim. *1 Samuel 14: v 41, 42* and *Exodus 28: v 30.*

Nobody is certain what the Urim and Thummim were. One idea is that they were two discs or stones which were kept in a pouch on the High Priest's chest. They were possibly black on one side and white on the other.

How could they have been used to simply answer questions by the word 'yes' or 'no'?

(*Clue:* throw colour same)

b The Casting of Lots. *Acts 1: v 23–26.*

A POSSIBLE EXPLANATION —The names of the two persons were marked on two stones of equal weight. Both stones were placed in a bowl and revolved until one came out. This stone would be God's choice.

2 What were the two most famous signs of protection the Hebrews ever used?

Read *Exodus 12: v 1–7, v 22–27,* also *Numbers 21: v 4–9.*

Signs of Faith

There are more different symbols of faith than perhaps any other. Here are but a few for you to consider.

1 The Masai medicine man always carried with him a 'sacred' bundle. This bundle was a small leather pouch which contained various oddments such as pieces of hair, some colourful stones, a few bones and, in recent times, even nuts and bolts. No one but the medicine man was allowed to look into the pouch or even to touch it. When the medicine man died the sacred bundle was passed on to his successor. In time the bag became a sign of magic power, and when a Masai tribesman was sick he would try to touch the pouch believing that it had a healing quality. A similar thing happened amongst the Cheyenne and Sioux Indians, and a Spanish Christian missionary named Cabeza de Vaca went about with a small cross which gave the sick Indians so much faith that the onlookers were amazed at the apparent healing qualities of what they called the 'magical' crossed sticks.

59

59 The thirteen Aztec day and night signs: the day signs have dots (at bottom and left). The night signs are above and right

73

2 Another strange sign of faith was the Cheyenne Indians' sacred hat and four arrows. The hat was a symbol of shelter and divine protection. Two of the arrows represented plentiful food and two signified victory in war. The arrows were thrown into the air and the shaman, after he had examined the position of these arrows on the ground, advised the tribe whether to attack an enemy or not. It could also be used to decide whether it was necessary to store food against the possibility of drought and famine.

3 The Navahos, like most Red Indian tribes, desperately wanted a vision from their guardian spirit. They took drugs and even suffered self torture in an effort to try to receive a vision. If eventually they had their vision and in it saw an elk or an eagle or any other creature, they would change their names and wear something representing the animal as a sign to others. In this way they hoped to show that the Great Father Spirit and their own guardian spirit had adopted them.

TASK C

1 Why would the Cheyenne use a hat as a symbol of shelter? (*Clue:* heat   summer)
2 One of the key signs of the Hebrew faith is to be found in *Exodus 20: v 9–10*. What is it?

62

60

Signs of Communication

Every sign can be a means of telling or reminding people of something, but some signs such as Indian smoke signals can be a way of talking.

The Sioux Indians had birds as their sign for prayer. This was because birds were the only things which they thought could take their messages up to Wakan Tanka, the Great Spirit who lived in the sky.

The most treasured sign of the Lango women of Uganda was a fertility tail which they wore to show that they were able to have babies.

This tail was most precious, but if a woman had done anything wrong it was taken from her and she was then seen by everyone to be in disgrace.

$\dot{\iota}\chi\theta\upsilon\varsigma$ – icthus – fish

ι	$\eta\sigma\upsilon\varsigma$	– Jesus
$\varkappa$	$\rho\iota\sigma\tau\upsilon\varsigma$	– Christ
θ	$\varepsilon\upsilon\upsilon$	– of God
υ	$\iota\upsilon\varsigma$	– son
σ	$\omega\tau\eta\rho$	– Saviour

61   AN IMPORTANT CHRISTIAN SIGN OF COMMUNICATION

A few years after Jesus had finally left the earth Christians became very unpopular with the Romans who tried to wipe out this new religion. After so many of the early Christians had been martyred, others had to be very secretive if they wanted to remain alive. The main problem was to decide how to recognise other Christians without giving themselves away to Roman spies. There is one possible way in which they may have done it. One Christian would draw the outline of a fish in the dust with his staff. Another Christian would recognise the sign and complete the drawing by placing the eye in the right place.

The sign of the fish may have been chosen because each letter of the Greek word for fish, ichthus, stood for the names: Jesus Christ, God, Son, Saviour, which may also have been an early creed or 'password' among Christians.

TASK D

1   Are there any other reasons why Christians may have used a fish as their secret sign? *(Clue: Read Luke 5: v 1–11)*.
2   Why was a candle often used as a sign? *Read Psalm 27: v 1; Exodus 10: v 23; Isaiah 60: v 1.*

Hebrew Signs and Symbols

Although the Hebrews never made statues of their God as most other people did, they still wanted to build a home for Him. The Temple was at the highest point in the heart of the city.

TASK E

1   Why was the Tabernacle so much simpler than the Temple? *(Clue:* place).
2   Read *Exodus 33: v 7–11;* and *2 Chronicles 3 and 4.*
    What were the main differences between the two places?
3   A wooden box called the Ark was placed in the tabernacle. Why was it so important to the Hebrews? *(Clue: Hebrews 9: v 3–5).*

Here are pictures of five different temples. All who built them were trying to show their devotion to their gods. In what way are they all alike? What were the worshippers trying to show in their buildings?

Jesus and His Signs

Jesus like everybody else used effective signs and symbols to emphasise some of His teaching. These signs can be seen not only in some of His stories but also by what He did. Here are a few examples:

1   The Parable of the Sower. *Mark 4: v 1–20.*
2   The Lamp. *Mark 4: v 21–25.*
3   The Mustard Seed. *Mark 4: v 30–32.*
4   Buried Treasure. *Matthew 13: v 44.*

TASK F

Try to find three more signs or symbols used by Jesus. *(Clue: St. John's Gospel.)*

IDEAS TO DEVELOP
Art and Craft

1   Design your own simple sign to show any of these important ideas:
   a   Peace
   b   Love
   c   Hope
   d   Industrial production
   e   Agriculture
   f   Co-operation
2   Make a mobile to show the four main things you have learnt about signs in this chapter.
   a   Use two wire coathangers.
   b   Cut off one hook, slip it over the end of the other coathanger so that they are at right angles to each other.
   c   Tie them together neatly with a piece of cotton.
   d   Paint pictures of the four things you have learnt about signs on four pieces of card 20 cm × 15 cm. Tie each one from a piece of cotton and hang them from the four corners of the mobile.
   e   Hang the mobile from the ceiling by a strong thread.

Chart

Make a large chart of symbols to represent four occasions in the Christian year:

1   Christmas. *Matthew 1: v 18; 2: v 12; Luke 2: v 1–20.*
2   Easter. *Matthew 27: v 1, 2, 27–44; 28: v 1–20; Mark 15: v 16–40; 16: v 1–7; Luke 23: v 18–49; 24: v 1–49.*
3   Whitsun. *Acts of the Apostles 2: v 1–11.*
4   Harvest Thanksgiving—This is similar to the Jewish Feast of the Tabernacles or Booths. *Leviticus 23: v 39–43.*

63

Diagrams

In *Exodus 25: v 10–22* and *Exodus 37: v 1–9* we are told how the Ark was made. Read the account and make a careful diagram of this great Hebrew symbol of God's presence.

(1 cubit = 45–50 cm.)

Living Language

1   Use these words in six sentences to show that you know what they mean:

sign   common   cult
apparent   guardian   communicate

2   The first words symbolise certain things—the other words are clues. Explain carefully in a short paragraph the connection between sign and clue.

a   Blood brothers: Indians, cut, blood, mix, friends.

b   Weather cock: coward, change. Read *Mark 14: v 66–72*.

c   Hammer and sickle: industry, farmer, together, a country.

d   Stars and stripes: stars, states, stripes, original states, Columbus found it.

e   Bulldog: power, determination, an island.

3   Imagine that you are living in a foreign country and cannot speak the language but you want to tell the story in *Luke 15: v 11–32* to somebody. Draw this story in signs.

4   Here is another short story shown in pictures.

64

What is the story about? You will find it between *Mark 2* and *Mark 6*.

Puzzles

Here are eight Christian signs. Pair them up with their correct meanings: glory, hope, sacrifice, gospel, worship, holiness, communion, suffering.

Library Work

Make a study of signs and symbols found in churches and cathedrals under the heading;

a   Buildings
b   Carvings
c   Ornaments

65

Further Research

65 Eight Christian signs
66 A rainbow

EITHER

Make a class booklet of some important signs and symbols used every day:

a   on roads
b   on railways
c   outside public houses
d   to indicate types of shops
e   as emblems of towns
f   on maps
g   as emblems of counties
h   as national emblems
i   as religious signs.

Your booklet can have eleven chapters—one to introduce the booklet, one chapter for each topic, and one to finish it.

OR`

Go to a local church and ask the minister why he wears:

A clerical dog collar.
A surplice.
A cassock.

66

Bible Research

1   What did the Hebrews think the rainbow signified? Read *Gen. 9: v 8–17.*

2   Why do women wear hats in church? Read *1 Corinthians 11: v 13–16.* (*Clue:* hide   humble).

3   The Ark was the Hebrew symbol of God's presence.
    What was put in it? See previous references to the Ark.
    How did it affect:
    Moses: *Exodus 25: v 22 and 30.*
    Aaron: *Leviticus 16: v 2.*
    Joshua: *Joshua 7: v 6.*
    Uzza: *2 Sam. 6: v 6 and 7.*
    Trace through the following references that show how the Ark affected the Hebrews.
    Deuteronomy 31: v 6–9; Joshua 3 and 4; Joshua 8: v 30–34; Judges 20: v 24–28; 1 Sam. 3: v 1–21; 4; 2 Sam. 7: v 1–13; 2 Sam. 15: v 24–29; 1 Kings 8: v 1–11; 2 Chronicles 35: v 3.
    Study closely the effect of the Ark on the Philistines from the following references: *1 Samuel 4, 5, 6: v 9.*

A Talk by Signs

Make up a short talk about any topic but it must be given by signs and no speaking is allowed except to introduce the topic.

Unit 8
A Growing Light

67

A fire, mist and a planet,
A crystal and a cell,
A jelly fish and a saurian,
The caves where cavemen dwell;
Then a sense of law and beauty
And a face turned from the clod,
Some call it evolution,
And others call it God.

William Herbert Carruth

We have now arrived at a position where we can see how the many puzzles of life and the seemingly unanswerable problems have caused almost the whole of mankind to hold religious beliefs. Of course these beliefs varied widely between nations and tribes but as religions developed they were used by leaders to make people act in special ways. Amongst such distant tribes as the Masai herders of East Africa and the Blackfoot Indians of America, it was the custom to split up into large family groups for most of the year, each held together only by their tribal religious beliefs. Once a year the family groups joined together for their religious dances before going their separate ways again. The Masai celebrated their sun dance at the beginning of a lion hunt. Similarly the Blackfoot celebrated their sun dance at the beginning of their buffalo hunt.

67 An Asanti chief and the stool of authority
68 Huitsilopochtali

68

Religious ideas have seldom progressed steadily as parts of this book seem to suggest. The primitive stages of animism, magic and ancestor worship did not evolve gradually from each other, but they often developed side by side. It is possible as we saw in Unit Two for the so-called civilised people of today to worship the machines of this scientific age and develop a modern animistic religion. Nevertheless it is possible to see how these primitive religious beliefs helped not only to unify the tribe but also to control it. For instance among the Aztec nation, the priests were the rulers and all wars were religious wars, in which they believed that their war-god, the Humming bird HUITSILOPOCHTALI, drove them on to victory over other gods. All of the nation's wealth and power was directed to fulfil this dominating national purpose. So too the Asanti tribe of Ghana used religion mainly to maintain law and order, because their faith demanded that every person should worship and respect their ancestors and elders. They had strange beliefs about chairs or stools. Whoever sat on a chief's chair was thought to share the god's authority and wisdom. Consequently Asanti leaders had replica stools which represented their authority. These stools had also belonged to their dead ancestors. Therefore young children carried their leaders' stools as they walked behind them and in so doing learnt how to respect the authority of their elders.

TASK A
Look at these references that show how religion:
a   unified the Hebrews
b   gave them a sense of purpose
c   helped them to maintain law and order
1   *Genesis 3 v 13–22; 1 Samuel 7: v 3–11; 1 Samuel 8: v 4–9.*
2   *Exodus 23: v 24–33; Exodus 24: v 3–8; Leviticus 20: v 6–9.*
3   *Exodus 20: v 3–17; 21: v 1–6; 21: v 7–11; 21: v 12–14; 21: v 15; 21: v 16; 21: v 17; 21: v 18–19; 21: v 20–21; 21: v 26–27; 21: v 28–32; ch. 22.*

Having studied them write a short composition on Hebrew religion

Man's Searching Spirit

The great strength of such religious convictions was the belief that life depended on something greater than the tribe or nation. People have always been restlessly searching for something greater than themselves and men have sacrificed the most valuable offerings in order to serve the Spirit which is 'greater than themselves', normally given the name 'God'.

An example of a man who possessed a remarkable searching spirit was Martin Luther. He was a Roman Catholic monk who lived in the sixteenth century, and is commonly regarded as the person who ignited the spark that began a great church REFORMATION. He spoke against the wicked practices of the church of his day. In spite of the persuasive measures taken by many of his friends and enemies to change his mind he refused to do so. He was asked by the church council to admit his mistakes in view of the threatened charge of heresy against him; a crime punishable by death in those days. His reply remains a permanent memorial to all who are willing to sacrifice even their lives for a principle which in all honesty they cannot deny. He said: 'Since then Your Majesty and your lordships desire a simple reply, I will answer without horns and without teeth. Unless I am convicted by Scripture and plain reason—I will not accept the authority of popes and councils, for they have contradicted each other—my conscience is captive to the word of God. I cannot and I will not recant anything, for to go against conscience in neither right—nor safe. God help me. Amen.'

It has always been impossible to be certain about things that cannot be seen and it is not surprising that the religious development of some tribes has been a story of fear amongst some and a story of faith amongst others.

Some of man's attempts to calm a guilty conscience and so be thought acceptable by the gods, seem very strange to us. For example, the guilt offering was one way in which the Hebrews tried to receive forgiveness. It has already been mentioned in Unit Four. The references already given to this guilt offering are: *Levit. 5: v 14–19* and *Levit. 7: v 1–7*.

Since food was often in short supply and men had to hunt for it in ancient days, it is not surprising to find that many of their

69 Martin Luther

82

70 Melanesian Islanders
sacrificing coconuts

sacrifices and thanksgiving festivals were mainly concerned with
food. The Melanesian Islanders of the South Pacific made the
priests bless the land and sharpen their digging sticks. They themselves offered sacrifices of coconuts to the spirit of the bonito fish
which they caught every year. In this way the Melanesians thought
that the spirits of beautiful sea maidens of the deep would guide
more bonito fish to the island.

Although some of these ancient beliefs in sacrificial thanks-giving seem horrific to our modern minds they were done for the most sincere, though often misguided reasons. This is clearly shown by the Maya Indians, who believed that they had to sacrifice not only their best young men and women but also many of their treasures by throwing them into a holy pit full of lime, to appease the Spirits. This was cruel but they, like so many other tribes, were only striving to satisfy their restless searching spirit.

All this has helped us to understand how early religious beliefs of various tribes helped:

a   to unify them
b   to solidify the nation with the notion of ancestor worship
c   to maintain law and order.

For instance, the Yoruba tribe held that certain land or property belonged to a family and the guardian spirits of that particular family would harm any who tried to take the land away from them.

Finally, religious beliefs provided tribes with a purpose in life. In the Old Testament the purpose of the desert wanderings of the Israelites was to allow them, when the time was ripe, to enter into the Promised Land. Look up this reference: *Exodus 3: v 7–8.*

TASK B

1   Read *Exodus 32: v 1–6* (Golden Calf). Why did the Israelites give all their gold to Aaron?
2   Read *Leviticus 23: v 39–44*. Why did the Israelites make these gifts to God? (Thanksgiving.)

The Hebrew Ideal

The Hebrews or Israelites, too, possessed this restless spiritual searching after God, but the one thing which made them different from other religious nations was the purity of their ideas. Their religious faith was born in Abraham who always looked forward in hope to better things and better times.

However, like people of so many faiths, the ordinary Hebrew people could not live up to these pure ideas, and great men, called 'prophets', had to come and call the Hebrews to return to the faith of their fathers. Men such as Moses and Elijah were not just holy men but men with a burning zeal that shook the people into repentance.

TASK C

Read *Exodus 32: v 15–26*. How did Moses shame the people to repentance?

Most of the Hebrew prophets stressed that the quality of a man's life was more acceptable to God than either human or any other kind of sacrifice. Man is described in the Old Testament as being 'made in God's image'. This not only meant to the Hebrew that man is able to tell right from wrong, but also since God is holy, righteous, good and merciful, a man must show that image by being kind and merciful in his daily life. The Hebrews only gradu-ally grew out of the idea that their God was a god of war and

punishment and came to realise that he was in truth the God of goodness.

TASK D

Look at these references and put them under one of these three appropriate headings:

a The Old Battle God.

b The God of War and Punishment.

c The Holy and Merciful God.

Psalm 24: v 8; Psalm 57: v 1; Psalm 75: v 7; Psalm 89: v 32; 2 Chronicles 7: v 13–17; Hosea 8: v 13.

Psalm 103: v 8; Amos 3: v 9–15; Exodus 15: v 6–13; Isaiah 13: v 9–11.

Levit. 11: v 44 and 45; Levit. 19: v 2; Hosea 11: v 9.

The Chosen Ones

In the same way that the Jewish priests were the middle men between their people and their God so too their nation, the Hebrew or Jewish nation, called Israel, was thought to be the 'middle man' between the true, living God and all the other nations of the world. They looked upon themselves as God's 'Chosen Vessel' and in some special way their God would choose from among them the Redeemer or Messiah. The whole of the Old Testament is the story of how God made a lasting Covenant or Agreement with the Hebrews. In short, it stated that He would be their God if they remained faithful to His commands. The Ten Commandments were the basis of their whole daily life and they marked out the Hebrews from their immediate surrounding neighbours. It seems unlikely that these laws were completely original but, like the ancient Babylonian laws of King Hammurabi, were probably the common code of the ancient Eastern world. However, these Laws were given a special significance by Moses; i.e. they were God's Laws.

72

TASK E

Look up these references which show how the Hebrews believed that they were the chosen Nation. What benefits and responsibilities resulted from this belief? *Exodus 4: v 22; Deut. 14: v 1 and 2; Deut. 32: v 3–12; Isaiah 1: v 2–4.*

Jesus the Chosen One

When the time was finally ripe Jesus of Nazareth was baptised in the river Jordan by His cousin John the Baptist and He then began to show the people a warmer and more personal side of God's character. In this book we have seen how Jesus is the Healer; the Messiah; the Mediator; the Final Sacrifice; the Victor over Death; the Son of the Father and finally the Sign of Salvation.

Jesus showed everybody what the Old Testament teaching had been leading up to, when He claimed that sin could be overcome through love and suffering. Not many really understood Him at the time because His teaching about God was so pure and so different from the traditional ideas of the Jewish religious teachers.

It is hoped that this book will cause you to think more about the person Jesus of Nazareth, whom Christians through the ages have claimed to be their Saviour.

IDEAS FOR DEVELOPMENT
Art and Craft
Religion, Nation, Law, Ancestor.

These four words suggest several stories in the unit.

Paint one of them.

Chart
Draw a chart which shows the four major effects of religion on a nation.

Cut four 18 cm squares of drawing paper.

Draw a simple picture in each square to show the effects.

Mount the illustrations on a sheet of black sugar paper and put a label in the centre.

73 Israel's ups and downs
74 Farmer, hunter, fisherman, herdsman

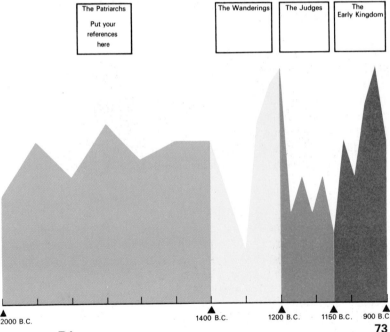

73

Diagram
Copy this simple graph which shows how the Hebrew religion progressed up to Solomon's time.

Look up the verses and print them in the correct squares:
Gen. 12: v 1–5; 12: v 10–20; 22: v 1–18; 26: v 17–25; Gen. 28: v 10–22; 50: v 24. Exodus 1: v 10–14; 14: v 21–31. Exodus 20: v 1–17. Josh. 24: v 19–25. Judges 2: v 11–15; 4: v 1–18; 6: v 1–6; 6: v 11–18; 20: v 42–48. 1 Sam. 7: v 13–16, ch. 31; 2 Sam. 23: v 1–5; 1 Kings 8: v 1–8, ch. 11.

Living Language

1 Write six sentences to show that you know what these words mean:

reform   celebrate   replica
ignite   maiden   image

2 Here is the first verse of a hymn by W. Charles Smith.
'Immortal, invisible God only wise,
In light inaccessible hid from our eyes.
Most blessed, most glorious, the Ancient of Days,
Almighty, victorious, Thy great name we praise.'

    a Use your dictionary to find the meaning of these words:
      immortal;   invisible;   inaccessible.

    b Write in your own words what the hymn writer was trying to say.

    c Does this agree with what the following believed?
      The Jews
      Jesus
      The Aztecs
      The Egyptians

3 Act the story of the Golden Calf in three short scenes.
(Exodus 32).

    a The Israelites become worried and talk to Aaron.

    b Making and worshipping the Golden Calf.

    c Moses' anger.

74

Deductive Work

From these four pictures, try to deduce the different types of religious beliefs of the:

a farmer
b hunter
c fisherman
d herdsman

Puzzle

These are parts of key words found in the chapter. Write the complete words out.

a - - nki - -   f - - res -   k - - rci - - -
b - - lie -   g - - ue -   l - ati - - -
c - - nc -   h - - int - - -   m - - vena - -
d - - air   i - ur -   n - ait -
e - eal - -   j - - cri - - - - o - - diat - -

75 Greek helmet
76 Christ on the cross

75

Library Work

1   What is a bonito fish?
2   Here are names of six Greek gods.
    Find out as much as you can about their purpose and write
    down in your own words a famous story associated with three
    of them.

Zeus   Hades   Athene
Hermes   Eros   Aphrodite
(*Dewey* 292.)

76

Further Research

Look around your town and find any activities which care for the
sick.
Make a list of them and find out exactly what they do.
Start with the branch of the Red Cross, and then go on to find out
about such activities as blood donating.
How does this tie up with Jesus's teaching:
'As much as ye do it unto one of these ye do it unto me'?

Bible Research

1   Look at these references and decide what is the main difference
    between the Hebrew and the Christian ideas of God.
    a   *Exodus 20: v 24*   cf: *1 Peter 2: v 4–5*.
    b   *Exodus 20 v 5*   cf: *Romans 11: v 1–6*.
    c   *Exodus 12: v 43*   cf: *1 Corinth. 12: v 12, 13*.
    d   *Job 4: v 17*.   cf: *Romans 4: v 5 and 6*.
    e   *Exodus 21: v 23–25*   cf: *Matt. 5: v 39–42*.
    f   *Levit. 19: v 18*   cf: *Matt. 5: v 44*.
2   Paul preached a sermon in Athens. To whom was a local altar
    dedicated? What did he tell the Athenians?
    Read Acts 17: v 22–34.

Discussion

Do you think that the Bible tells the story of God looking for man
or of man looking for God?

Unit 9
Review

The eight units in this book show how people have gradually learnt about God. Here are some interesting ways of revising all the work.

1 Look at this list of some of the tribes and nations mentioned in this book. Let each class group collect all the information together about a different tribe or nation.

Manus	Babylonians	Incas	Egyptians
Mayas	Aztecs	Sherpas	Eskimos
Masai	Aborigines	Asanti	Assyrians
Red Indians	Balinese		

2 Are these statements true or false?
   a An animist is a person who thinks gods are like animals.
   b Elijah was a Biblical witch doctor.
   c The Messiah releases mankind from suffering.
   d The priests did not want to be cruel when they sacrificed human beings to gods.
   e A terebinth was a sacred tree.
   f All priests foretold the future.
   g Sacrifices were only made to have sins forgiven.
   h A scapegoat was offered as a sacrifice on the Day of Atonement.
   i The Hebrews were a patriarchal society.
   j Hebrew children could be killed for disobedience.

3 One eight circles of white drawing paper, each with a radius of 10 cm, draw and paint eight pictures. Let each one sum up one of the eight units. Mount them on two sheets of sugar paper.

4 Draw a large map of the world or trace a wall map.
   Mark the position of the tribes and nations on the map, and in small squares on the map draw pictures which sum up the religious beliefs of the tribes.

5 Draw up a series of ten statements from the units which could come under the heading 'Strange but True'.

6 To whom do these phrases refer?
   a He learned how to forecast the weather from signs in the sky.
   b He did the same kinds of things as the medicine man.
   c They caused the crops to reappear and produce a harvest.
   d They took drugs and even suffered self torture to try to receive a vision.
   e He was not only a father, a priest and a judge to his family but he was also the one who taught his own trade to his sons.

f They thought it was sinful for children to fight.

g He thought all his property belonged to the dead members of his family, as well as the living ones.

7 What did the book tell you about the following people in the Bible?

Abraham   Moses   Elijah   Jesus

8 Locate these verses:

a I will make you fishers of men.

b In the beginning God . . .

c Get thee out of thy country . . . unto a land that I will show thee.

d Thou shalt not make unto thee any graven image.

e The Lord is my Shepherd.

f The kingdom of heaven is like a grain of mustard seed.

g Ye are the salt of the earth; the light of the world.

h Thou art old, and thy sons walk not in thy ways, nor make us a king to judge us like all nations.

i I have commanded the ravens to feed thee there.

j He made his son pass through the fire, and observed times and used enchantments, and dealt with familiar spirits and wizards.

77

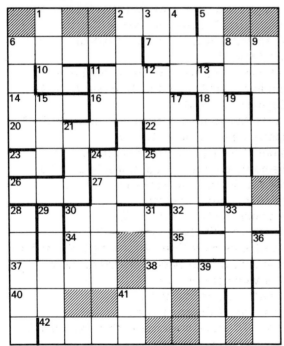

9 Solve this crossword puzzle after drawing it in your work book. Each square is 1 cm.

CLUES

Across

  2   A backward sun?

  6   An eskimo goddess.

  7   Prophets by another name. *1 Sam. 9: v 9.*

10   The New Testament in short.

11   The father of the Hebrews.

77 The empty tomb

14   A disciple cut this off. *Mark 14: v 47.*
16   Jesus met two followers on the . . . to Emmaus. *Luke 24.*
18   The Old Testament.
20   An Eskimo born in the summer.
22   The great law-giver.
23   . . . thou be the Son of God. *Luke 4: v 3.*
24   The people did this at Jericho. *Joshua 6: v 5.*
26   A Cheyenne symbol of shelter.
27   The pyramids were gigantic . . .
30   A nation of religious Indians in Central America.
32   Incas inspected this for guidance.
34   Abraham lived there. *Genesis 11.*
35   More than just bad.
37   The Egyptians had thousands of these.
38   Jesus gave 5,000 people a . . . *Mark 6: v 37.*
40   O give thanks unto the Lord; for he . . . good. *Psalm 118: v 1.*
41   Short for the book of Isaiah.
42   This word is in *Isaiah 55: v 13.*

Down

 1   An uncomfortable bedroom. *Daniel 6: v 16.*
 2   He owned a vineyard. *1 Kings 21: v 1.*
 3   Forgive . . . our Trespasses. *Luke 11: v 4.*
 4   Moses took the Israelites across the Red . . . *Exodus 14: v 16.*
 5   A short name for a person (man). *Mark 4: v 1.*
 6   Jesus told a parable about it. *Matthew 13: v 31.*
 8   The Egyptian sun god.
 9   Moses did this to the tablets on which were the Ten Commandments. *Exodus 32: v 19.*
11   A symbol of God's presence. *Exodus 37: v 1.*
12   Abraham offered this to God. *Genesis 22: v 13.*
13   God was sometimes called the Lord of . . .
15   An Egyptian word for corpse.
17   Twice as much. *Genesis 43: v 12.*
19   God did this to Abraham. *Genesis 22.*
21   This word is found in *Mark 14: v 47* (R. S. Version).
24   The Egyptians and Babylonians studied these.
25   Part of a Vedic prayer.
28   Some witch doctors did this.
29   The most sacred Christian symbol.
30   Pharaoh's chariots were stuck in this. *Exodus 14.*
31   Battles were fought with these.
33   An Egyptian river.
36   Jesus' teaching about God. *1 John 4: v 8.*
39   A weapon. *Matthew 3: v 10.*
41   The very first word in the Bible.

10   Discuss the following:

   a   He cleans and polishes his car as if it were his god.
   b   It is no longer necessary to sacrifice to God.
   c   If strangers came from space do you think they would have any religious ideas?

Book List

Book List and Visual Aids

220.3 C. Northcott *Bible Encyclopaedia for Children* (Lutterworth)

292 R. Warner *Men and Gods* (Heinemann) A well written book about Greek gods and goddesses, useful for private reading

220.9 N. B. Keyes *Story of the Bible World in Maps, Word and Picture* (Oldbourne) A good source book for Bible background material

220.9 M. T. Gilbertson *The Way it was in Bible Times* (Lutterworth) A good summary of customs, homes and temples

922 N. J. Bull *Great Christians Series* (4 vols) (Hulton) A good reference series for stories about martyrs, missionaries and heroes. Each chapter has a section on 'Questions' and 'Things to Do'

220.3 D. S. Daniels and E. W. H. Lampe *The Discovery Reference Book—Discovering the Bible* (U.L.P.) A good book on 'How the Bible Came to Us'

929 J. O. Evans *The Observer's Book of Flags* (Warne) Useful for Unit 7—Speaking Without Words

973 T. A. Thompson *Blackwell's Learning Library—Red Indians* (Blackwell)

720.9 A. Gibson *Homes of The World* (Chatto & Windus) Useful for Unit 6—Under One Roof

220.8 H. I. Rostron *Animals, Birds and Plants of the Bible* (Ladybird)

728 J. Morey *Let's Look at Houses and Homes* (Muller)

922 *Missionaries* (short biographies) (E.H.P.)

   A. G. Cartleton *On the Roof of the World—Pollard of China*

   M. B. Rix *Mary and the Black Warriors—Mary Slessor of Africa*

   P. Yates *Apolo in Pygmyland—Carson Apolo of Uganda*

   M. Entwistle *Where White Men Died—Crowther of Africa*

296 S. R. Weilerstein *Ten and a Kid* (World's Work) A good book on the Jewish family life and religious festivals

932 E. Payne *All About the Pharaohs* (W. H. Allen)

932 L. Cottrell *Land of the Pharaohs* (Brockhampton)

935 L. Cottrell *Land of the Two Rivers* (Brockhampton)

572 S. Blacker *The Masai—Herders of East Africa* (Dobson)

972 V. W. von Hagen *The Sun King of the Aztecs* (Brockhampton)

985 V. W. von Hagen *The Incas—People of the Sun* (Brockhampton)

985 C. A. Burland *Finding Out About the Incas* (Muller)

948 D. Phillips-Birt *Finding Out About the Vikings* (Muller)

935 E. R. Pike *Finding Out About the Babylonians* (Muller)

972 C. Gallencarp *Finding Out About the Maya* (Muller)

972 W. H. Jordan and E. R. Pike *Finding Out About the Aztecs* (Muller)

919.4 R. Rose *Living Magic* (Chatto & Windus)

972 J. E. Thompson *The Rise and Fall of the Maya Civilisation* (Gollancz)

571 G. Grigson *The Painted Caves* (Phoenix)

571 A. & G. Sieve King *The Caves of France and North Spain* (Vista Books)

133 J. Maringer *The Gods of Prehistoric Man* (Weidenfeld & Nicolson)

916 International Affairs Institute *African Worlds* (O.U.P.)

133.4 M. Deren *The Living Gods of Haiti* (Thames & Hudson)

290 *The World's Great Religions* (Collins)

220.9 G. E. Wright *Biblical Archaeology* (Duckworth)

913 *The Golden Book of Lost Worlds* (Golden Press)

225 A. C. Bouquet *Everyday Life in N.T. Times* (Batsford)

221 E. W. Heaton *Everyday Life in O.T. Times* (Batsford)

220 T. W. Wilson *Through the Bible* (Collins)

220 E. B. Reddish *Let's Look at the Bible* (Weldons)

220 *Hoolbutt's Story of the Bible* (Ward Lock)

220.3 *The New Bible Dictionary* (I.V.F.)

220.7 *Peake's Commentary* (Nelson)

933 J. Bright *History of Israel* (S.C.M.)

221 B. W. Anderson *The Living World of the Old Testament* (Longman)

221 A. C. Kee and F. W. Young *The Living World of the New Testament* (Darton)

221 E. A. Nida *Custom, Culture and Christianity* (Tyndale)

Visual Aids

Here are a few of the visual aids which will help to improve your projects.

Type of material	Title	Colour or Black/white	Running Time	Source
Film	Rivers of Time	Colour	25 m.	Petroleum Film Bureau
Filmstrip	Bible Scrolls FF85,86	Colour	60 frames	Concordia Films
Filmstrip	Bible Cities	Colour	58 frames	Concordia Films
Filmstrip	Abraham CP-150	Colour	27 frames	Concordia Films
Filmstrip	Jacob CP-151	Colour	42 frames	Concordia Films
Filmstrip	Joseph CP-152, 153	Colour	67 frames	Concordia Films
Filmstrip	Moses CP-154, 155	Colour	81 frames	Concordia Films
Filmstrip	Elijah CP-163	Colour	42 frames	Concordia Films
Filmstrip	David CP-160, 161	Colour	64 frames	Concordia Films
Slides	The Living Bible Series	—	6 slides	Concordia Films
Slides	Miracles of Jesus CS.F	—	6 slides	Concordia Films
Film	2000 Years Ago Series	Black/white		Rank
	The School		20 m.	
	The Synagogue		20 m.	
	Day's Work		20 m.	
	Home		20 m.	
Film	Bible Background	Black/white	50 m.	Rank
Filmstrip	The Epic of Man Series: 　The Dawn of Religion 　Coming of Civilisation 　First Great Civilisation 　Oldest Nation: Egypt 　Egypt's Eras of Splendour 　Homeric Greece 　The Celts	Colour	56 frames	Life Magazine
Filmstrip	The World We Live In: 　Ancient Egypt 　Athens 　Peking 　Heritage of the Maya 　The Incas	Colour	56 frames	Life Magazine

Films and Filmstrips

Religious Films of all kinds are available from the following:

SPCK Films Dept.,
Holy Trinity Church, Marylebone Road, London, N.W.1.

The Church Army, Visual Aid Dept.,
185 Marylebone Road, London, N.W.1.

Concordia Films,
117-123 Golden Lane, London, E.C.1.

Religious Education Press,
Wallington, Surrey.

Warner Pathe, (*Journey of a Lifetime* Series),
Wardour Street, London, W.1.

Educational Foundation for Visual Aids,
33 Queen Anne Street, London, W.1.

Religious Films Ltd.,
6 Eaton Gate, London, S.W.1.

Fact and Faith Films,
26a Warren Drive, Wallasey, Cheshire.

Life Magazine,
Time & Life Buildings, Rockefeller Center, New York 10020.

Index

To The Teacher

This is the first of a series of books of religious education which are aimed at a broad range of ability in secondary schools. They have been written to cover the requirements of the secondary school up to examination year. Each book is an entity though there are strong links forward and backward to other volumes.

Taken as a whole, this course provides a broad and sound background of religious knowledge even for examination candidates. At the same time, the theme of each book is parallel to those of the other subjects in the series.

This volume, *From Fear to Faith*, is intended as a bridge between the work of the junior and the secondary stages. It attempts to show the various forms of primitive belief all over the world, relating particularly to the peoples described in the corresponding geography book of this series. From these beliefs, the book traces the development towards a religion which has replaced fear by faith.

Each unit consists of an illustrated narrative broken at intervals by short tasks. Following this is a considerable section headed *Ideas to Develop* in which the pupil's own efforts are encouraged. These sections include work in Living Language, Facts and Figures, Art and Craft, Geography, as well as Mapwork, Library Work, Biblical Research, and Discussion Themes.

These books are intended as aids to the teacher, not to reduce his importance. The great range of ideas, activities, and projects means that all pupils can be fully occupied while the teacher gives group or individual attention when and where necessary. To help in the planning there are full lists of aids and books relevant to each unit. Their use, combined with the book and the teacher's own abilities, provides an exciting series of studies.